The Master's Cabinet

Lives Of Faith And Service

Robert L. Allen

CSS Publishing Company, Inc., Lima, Ohio

THE MASTER'S CABINET

For more information about CSS Publishing Company resources, visit our website at www.csspub.com or e-mail us at custserv@csspub.com or call (800) 241-4056.

ISBN 0-7880-2309-8   PRINTED IN U.S.A.

This book is dedicated to
Joe Prothro,
a man of faith who is
a friend and "pastor" to me.

Table Of Contents

Preface

The Presidential election of 2000 was one of the most controversial elections in our nation's history. Eventually, the contested election was settled with a ruling by the U.S. Supreme Court.

During the campaign for the 2000 election, each candidate began to leak to the news agencies who their appointments would be to various Cabinet positions. The members of the Cabinet are selected by the newly-elected President to run the agencies of our government and serve as his closest advisors.

Have you ever wondered about those who were selected to serve in the Master's Cabinet? Jesus selected twelve individuals to be his traveling companions ... to be his confidants ... to be his disciples.

These twelve disciples came from a variety of backgrounds. Some were fishermen. Some were tax collectors. Some belonged to a radical revolutionary group called the Zealots. And Jesus called them to leave whatever they were doing and join him in his ministry. His call was simple and clear: "Follow me and I will make you fish for people."

As you read through this book, you will have a chance to see the enormous debt of gratitude that we owe to these men who served in the Master's Cabinet. They faced a lot of abuse, criticism, and even persecution. Yet, all but one of the twelve remained faithful to Jesus even unto death. Had it not been for this group of men and their willingness to take up their cross and tell the story of God's love in Jesus Christ, our understanding of God and our relationship to God would be very different.

Robert L. Allen

Andrew:
A Second-String Outfielder

John 1:40-42; 6:8-9; 12:20-22

In the spring of the year, baseball begins to dominate the sports headlines. Sports writers begin speculating about who will lead the league in home runs. Fans wonder if anyone will win the Triple Crown and lead the league in batting average, home runs, and RBIs. Fans begin to wonder if their favorite team has a chance of making the playoffs and perhaps going to the World Series. And the owners of certain teams decide that their team has no chance for the playoffs and start trading veteran players for younger players who are not stars yet, but have the potential of becoming superstars.

These trades of star players for players with star potential sometimes involve money. And sometimes a trade involves a "second-string outfielder." This "second-string outfielder" is not a star making a huge salary. He is relegated to the bench. He only gets in the game when someone is injured. He is a second-string outfielder and not expected to be a star.

And this is the way it was with the disciple named Andrew. He was never one of the stars among the disciples. Most of us know almost nothing about Andrew except that he was Simon Peter's brother and one of the twelve that Jesus chose to follow him. Apparently, he had none of the charisma that Peter possessed. He was much more even-tempered than the Sons of Thunder, James and John. He was an ordinary fellow, the kind of person we come in contact with every day. He might sit in the pew next to us or carry our mail or wait on us in a store or work at the next desk.

From what we can gather, Andrew never became a star and he seemed content to play second string to all of the other disciples. All that mattered was that he was a follower of Jesus.

Even though Andrew was never a star, there is no doubt that his relationship to Jesus Christ was the most significant event in his life. Andrew was a simple fisherman from Bethsaida. He was a follower of John the Baptist, and it was this relationship that directed him to Jesus. There was something about Jesus that caught Andrew's attention. Perhaps it was the air of authority about his personality. Perhaps it was the compassion in his heart. Perhaps it was the sense of God's presence in Jesus.

Whatever it was, Andrew became convinced that Jesus was the Messiah and decided to follow him. His commitment to Jesus was so intense that even though he always seemed to be on the second string, he wanted others to know Jesus. Andrew appears only three times in the Gospels and each time he is introducing someone to Jesus. First, he brought his brother, Simon Peter, and introduced him to Jesus. Next, he found a little boy with five loaves of bread and two fish and he brought the boy to Jesus. This encounter made possible the feeding of the 5,000. Finally, some people from Greece asked Philip to introduce them to Jesus, Philip referred them to Andrew, and he promptly took them and introduced them to Jesus.

In Christian history, Andrew never became a star. He always seemed to play the role of a second-string outfielder. Yet, he seems to have accepted that role with the best of grace because he was committed to Jesus Christ.

I want to suggest that many of us are like Andrew. We are not stars in his kingdom, but ordinary people who can be used by God. There are three ideas I want us to consider.

1. God Uses Second-String Outfielders Because They Are Important.

Andrew seemed to play second string to his brother and all of us know how difficult it is to be second. It is not easy to live out your life day after day, week after week, year after year. It is not easy being in a subordinate position while somebody else gets the notice, the publicity, the attention, the credit, the praise, the spotlight, and perhaps the reward. It takes a lot of grace always to be second. It takes a lot of humility to be understanding in the face of those who play the more prominent roles.

I like the little story that I read recently about a little boy who took the family basset hound, Pluto, to enter a dog show. When he returned home, his mother asked how it went at the dog show.

"Great!" the little boy said. "Pluto got second place in best of the breed."

"I'm very proud," said the mother. "How many basset hounds were entered in the dog show?"

"Two," the little boy replied.

Being in second place does not diminish our value and worth. We are important simply for who we are, and God can use us for his kingdom.

In the summer of 1955, a black woman, who worked as a maid, knew that her lot in life did not have much of a chance of improving. With very little education and training, she knew deep in her heart that she was not likely to have a prominent place in the affairs of the world.

One day she got off work and she was especially tired and exhausted. When the bus pulled up and she climbed up the steps, her usual spot at the back of the bus was taken. There were empty seats at the front of the bus, but the law in 1955 in Birmingham, Alabama, required her to go to the back of the bus.

But, Rosa Lee Parks was tired and it didn't make sense for her to stand at the back of the bus when she could sit at the front. So, she found a seat at the front and sat down. The driver asked her to move, but she refused. The police were called and she was arrested. That evening the Civil Rights movement was on its way to affirming that everyone — red or yellow, black or white — was important and entitled to be treated equally and with dignity.

And what was the impetus of the Civil Rights movement? It wasn't an inspiring speech by Martin Luther King, Jr., or Jesse Jackson. It was a black maid who believed that she should be treated fairly and with dignity.

In God's kingdom and throughout all of life, most of us will never be stars. The best we may ever do is to be second-string outfielders who play small parts, but God can still use us for his purposes because we are important.

2. God Uses The Second-String Outfielder To Get His Work Done.

Andrew was not one of the greatest disciples, but he was one who was willing to do his part. Without Andrew and all of the other second-stringers in God's kingdom, the work and will of God could not be accomplished. And God uses people like Andrew. God uses people like you and me.

There is a famous statue in a church in Berlin. It is Thorwaldsen's statue of Christ with his arms outstretched. During the bombings of World War II, this statue was damaged. The explosion of a bomb had broken off the arms. Many people thought this great piece of art was totally ruined. It seemed pitiful to look into the handsome, pleading face of Jesus, chiseled in beautiful white marble, and note that he had no arms to reach out and bless people.

But, this is really a more accurate portrayal of Jesus. The only hands that he has to bless the world are our hands. The only feet he has to go into all the world are our feet. The only voice he has to speak and proclaim his love is our voice. We are his hands, his feet, his voice, and his witnesses.

The future of the kingdom of God depends largely upon the Andrews of the world, the second-string outfielders who do God's work with little thought of recognition. I believe that Jesus has chosen you and me, just as he chose Andrew, to do his work in the world. Are you doing your part? Are you doing anything for God? Are you willing to play second string, if need be, in order that God's work can be accomplished?

The work of God needs to be done and if it is to be completed, it is up to the ordinary men and women in the church — like you and me!

3. God Uses The Second-String Outfielder To Bring People To Jesus.

Every time Andrew appears on the New Testament scene, he is introducing someone to Jesus. Andrew developed a knack of introducing people to Jesus. He introduced his brother, Simon Peter, to Jesus. He brought the boy with the five barley loaves and two fish which enabled Jesus to feed the 5,000. He took some Greeks who were in town for the Passover and introduced them to Jesus.

It is all right to be impressed with the contributions of great religious leaders in the church. They do many great things. They do them well. They receive the publicity, praise, and reward. But, there are a host of ordinary men and women who never get their names printed in the papers or their faces on television, but in their own quiet and unassuming way they carry out the work of the church by introducing their friends, neighbors, co-workers, and relatives to Jesus Christ.

I know of a Methodist minister who did not attend Sunday school or church very much as a young boy. His parents were not anti-religious; they simply preferred to sleep in on most Sundays. Consequently, as a young boy he attended Sunday school and church very infrequently.

When he was about eleven years old, a new Sunday school teacher took over his class. Every Saturday, this new teacher would call everyone in his class and say, "I'm looking forward to seeing you in Sunday school tomorrow ..." Each month he would take the boys and girls in his class to the skating rink or bowling alley or fishing. He loved and cared for each child in his class. He would visit them in their homes if they missed three Sundays in a row. He thought it was important for each boy and girl in his class to know something about God's love in Jesus Christ.

The name of that Sunday school teacher is long since forgotten by the world. But, it is written down in the Lamb's Book of Life because God used an obscure and unknown Sunday school teacher to introduce young boys and girls to Jesus Christ. God used an unknown Sunday school teacher to challenge boys and girls to commit their lives to him. God used an unknown, second-string Sunday school teacher to touch the lives of boys and girls with the Good News of God's love in Jesus Christ. And, over a period of fifteen years as a Sunday school teacher, eleven boys and girls felt the call of God into the ministry.

One Methodist minister said, "I owe my call to the ministry to that Sunday school teacher who cared about me."

A Methodist missionary said, "I owe my faith to a Sunday school teacher who thought it was important for him to introduce me to Jesus Christ."

Are you doing your part in the kingdom of God? Have you invited anyone to your Sunday school class? Have you invited anyone to sing in the choir with you?

The whole business of the church and God's kingdom depends upon people like Andrew — the second-string outfielders, the obscure and unknown disciples, the people who quietly live out their faith each day, the people who may never stand in the pulpit or become missionaries — but, because they love and care about their friends, they take them and introduce them to Jesus Christ.

Jesus may not call you to be a missionary who crosses the sea, but he may call you to cross the street and invite a friend or neighbor to your church.

Jesus knew what he was doing when he chose Andrew to be one of his disciples. He may not have been one of the superstars among the disciples. He may have only been a second-string outfielder, but Jesus knew that Andrew could make a difference as one of his disciples.

And, just as Jesus chose Andrew to be one of his disciples, he is choosing you. Jesus is calling you, just as he called to Andrew: "Follow me and I will make you fish for people" (Matthew 4:19 NRSV).

Jesus is calling to you! Will you hear that call? Will you dare to follow him? What will you say as Jesus calls you?

Prayer

O God, help us to hear your call in our lives. Enable us to know that we can make a difference in your kingdom by living our faith each day. In his name. Amen.

Matthew:
When Others Reject You

Matthew 9:9-13

A few years ago, I had an unusual thing happen in my church. A young couple, planning to get married in my church, had reserved the church and put their wedding on our calendar. I had a couple of counseling sessions with them. The wedding announcements had been mailed. They had arranged for a florist and a caterer. The bride had purchased a wedding gown. The bridesmaid dresses were being made.

Everything seemed to be set for this couple to have a lovely wedding and begin sharing their lives together as husband and wife.

Then, just a couple of weeks before this wedding, a young woman called the church, identified herself as the bride, cried a little on the phone, and informed the secretary that the wedding was being cancelled and we could give that June date to another bride.

Well, I can tell by the grins on some of your faces that you are way ahead of me. The young woman who called to cancel the wedding was not the bride who scheduled the wedding. She was the groom's ex-fiancée, and she was trying to create a problem.

Fortunately, my secretary caught the duplicity before a conflict developed. But, there is something within each one of us that understands the ex-fiancée. She had been rejected and hurt and she was trying to get even.

There is something within each of us that knows what it is to experience rejection. Yet, every last one of us knows what it is to be rejected. This is obvious in life. It is obvious in literature. It is obvious even in the Bible.

When you read the story of Matthew, you are reading about a man who knew what it was to be rejected. Matthew was a tax collector for the Romans, and the Jews considered him to be a quisling, a collaborator, a traitor who betrayed his own people.

It wasn't just Matthew who was hated, but all Jews who collected taxes for the Romans. They collected taxes from their own people, deducted a hefty percentage as their own fee, and gave the balance to the Romans.

Matthew and all tax collectors knew what it was to be rejected. Their word was worthless in court. Men would shun them on the streets or in the Temple. They were *persona non grata* or unwelcome at social functions. Their money was unacceptable in the synagogue. No one showed any concern for their problems. They were considered to be reprobates and classified with the harlots and other sinners.

Yes, Matthew knew what it was to be rejected, and so do we. We want to be liked and included with others, but we have encountered those situations where we are not accepted. It is painful when you feel that you are being ignored. It is a miserable experience to feel that you do not fit in and that you could just walk away and no one would notice. It hurts deep inside when you know that others just do not care for you. We understand rejection because we've experienced rejection. We know what it is like to feel the rejection of others.

The real question about rejection is not whether we are going to experience it, but how are we going to respond. There have been times in our past and there will be occasions in our future when we are rejected. How will we respond? Will we allow the hurt to overwhelm us?

Or, will we learn how to deal with it effectively?

There are three things I think are important in dealing with the idea of rejection, which we all experience at one time or another.

1. When Others Reject You, Don't Hold A Grudge.

When someone rejects us, it hurts and we have a natural tendency to want to get even. The anger and hurt take root in our hearts and soon it blossoms into a healthy grudge. This grudge takes up residence in our hearts and minds, and we spend our time wanting to get even. We spend our time plotting revenge. We spend our time trying to figure out how we can hurt them as badly as we have been hurt.

There was a woman who was bitten by a dog suspected of having rabies. She was rushed to the hospital, treated, and left in a room to wait for an autopsy report on the dog. Only then would she know if she had to take the series of shots for rabies. An intern on duty thought he should explain the seriousness of the situation to the woman. He told her all the dangers of rabies and she asked him a lot of questions. By the time he finished, he realized that he had told her more than he had meant to tell her because the woman was visibly shaken at the prospect of having rabies.

The intern was called from the room and when he returned, she was sitting on the treatment table with a legal pad in her hand and she was writing. She would pause for a moment, stare out into space, then resume writing.

The young intern was sure that he had frightened her and she was making out her will. He went back into the examining room to talk with her. He asked her, "Are you making out your will?"

"No!" she said. "Just in case I have been infected with rabies, I'm making a list of the people I want to bite before I die."

We all know that holding a grudge and plotting revenge is not a healthy response. When we hold a grudge and plot revenge against one who has rejected us and hurt us, we are lowering ourselves to their level.

When others reject you and hurt you, I believe that the appropriate response is not in holding a grudge, but in forgiving. It isn't easy to forgive when you are hurting on the inside. It isn't easy to forgive when the seeds of anger and bitterness are sprouting in your heart. It isn't easy to let go of the pain. But, forgiveness is the only appropriate response.

Recently, I have been reading some about Pope John Paul II. He will be remembered as a significant figure in the Catholic Church. Shortly after an attempt to assassinate him, the mother of his would-be assassin showed up at the Vatican unannounced and asked to see the Pope. During her short meeting with the Pope, she asked him if he would forgive her son for trying to assassinate him. The Pope replied, "I forgave him shortly after the attempt on my life."

The newsman reporting on the meeting at the Vatican closed his report by saying, "I suppose it is the Pope's business to forgive."

Well, it is the business of every last one of us to forgive. It may not be easy to forgive, but I believe that it is the only way to overcome the hurt, the anger, the bitterness, and the pain when others reject us.

2. When Others Reject You, Don't Reject Yourself.

Often, when we have been rejected by others, we have a tendency to reject ourselves. We think that we deserve to be hurt and rejected by others. We think that there is something wrong with our lives — after all, others must be rejecting us for some reason.

I have seen people who have been so hurt by rejection that they start rejecting themselves. They do this by pulling a defensive curtain around themselves and shutting others out. By isolating themselves, they are avoiding the hurt of being rejected by others, but they are rejecting themselves.

Often in children's homes we see children who have been abused and rejected by their families. They are so hurt by this rejection that they are afraid to be loving and trusting of anyone. It is as if they are saying, "I will not risk being rejected ever again!"

Therefore, they either behave in ways that keep others away or they isolate themselves in their own little prisons. They are afraid of being hurt. They are afraid of being rejected. So they act in ways that destroy any chance of being close to others.

So, in the name of everything worthwhile, don't reject yourself. Every one of us knows what it is to be hurt and rejected, but always remember that you are someone who is unique. You are a special creation of God. There is no one else in the world who is exactly like you.

I am not trying to inflate your ego or whitewash your mistakes. I am simply trying to get you to see that when God made you, God made someone who is special, and you need to realize how special you are. You need to realize that there is no one else in

18

this whole world who is exactly like you.

Once I heard of a little girl who went to play with a friend of hers named Melissa. When she rang the doorbell, an older sister answered the door and said, "Melissa said that she didn't want to play."

Then, the little girl standing at the door said to her friend's older sister, "Melissa will want to come outside and play when she knows that it is me."

Now, that may be a little presumptuous, but I hope that child never loses her sense of security, that sense of being someone special, that sense of being unique.

After all, we are all unique creations of God. There is something worthwhile about each of us and we don't need to be rejecting ourselves. We simply need to learn that we are, indeed, special creations of God and we should be tolerant with ourselves.

3. When Others Reject You, Remember That God Chooses You.

A young man and woman had been going together for a long time. One night as they were parked on a hilltop with the convertible top down and looking up at the moon, the young man decided to propose. He said, "Darling, I want you to know that I love you more than anything in the world. I'm not like Jimmy Green. I'm not wealthy. I'm not rich. I don't own a condo in Colorado or a beach house on Padre Island like Jimmy Green. But I love you with all my heart and I want you to marry me."

The girl was silent for a moment and then she said, "Can you tell me a little more about Jimmy Green?"

Others may reject us and hurt us throughout our lives, but God always chooses us. Others may shun us and want nothing to do with us, but God always chooses us. Others may ignore us and bring pain to our lives, but God always accepts us with open arms.

The other disciples must have stood with their mouths open in astonishment the day Jesus said to Matthew, "Follow me." He was despised and hated because he was a tax collector. He had no close friends. He lived a life that was oriented around material values. He knew what it was to be rejected and despised and ignored by the common people.

But Jesus still chose him. One of the most dramatic verses in all scripture is: "Jesus left that place, and as he walked along, he saw a tax collector, named Matthew, sitting in his office. He said to him, 'Follow me.' Matthew got up and followed him" (Matthew 9:9 TEV).

I wonder if we will ever catch the full impact of those verses. Matthew was despised by everyone in the community. Matthew was hated by most of the people. Matthew was rejected by most of the people. But, Jesus still chose Matthew.

This is the gospel we need to hear today. We may be rejected, we may be despised, we may be alone and isolated in our world. But God still chooses us. God still calls us to be his disciples.

You may have been rejected by everyone in this world. But, the Good News is that God still chooses you. God still calls you to follow him. God still loves you, even when others reject you. God still chooses you through his Son, Jesus Christ.

Prayer

O God, there are times when we feel rejected and we hurt inside our hearts. Help us to know that you never reject us, but you always choose us because of your love for us in Jesus Christ. In his name. Amen.

Thomas:
The Disciple From Missouri

John 20:24-29

In the Broadway play, *My Fair Lady*, Eliza Doolittle sings "Don't talk of stars burning above, if you're in love, show me!"

She wanted proof that the love was real. She wasn't going to believe simply because of some romantic words. She wanted to be shown.

This is the way it was with Thomas. He was a good man and one of the most loyal and devoted men who joined Jesus' group of disciples. Just like the other disciples, he left his home, he left his family, he left his job, and he left everything behind to become one of the disciples who served in the Master's Cabinet.

Traveling with Jesus had an impact on Thomas. He sat at the feet of the Master and listened to his words of wisdom. When Jesus heard that Lazarus was ill and he was going to return to Jerusalem, the other disciples tried to talk him out of it because he might be killed. Yet, it was Thomas who said, "Let us go and die with him ..." (John 11:16). He was the only disciple willing to risk his life with Jesus.

We know Thomas was sometimes confused about the teachings of Jesus. When Jesus sought to assure his disciples by saying, "Let not your hearts be troubled ... In my Father's house are many rooms ... I go to prepare a place for you ... And you know the way where I am going ..." (John 14:1-4 RSV). It was Thomas who expressed the confusion that the other disciples felt. He said: "Lord, we do not know where you are going; how can we know the way?" (Matthew 14:5 RSV).

However, the one incident that everyone remembers about Thomas took place after the Easter miracle. Thomas was not present with the other disciples. He had watched his Master die. He saw the nails driven through the flesh. He saw the spear pierce his side. He saw Jesus taken down from the cross and buried in the borrowed tomb of Joseph of Arimathea.

Thomas went off to grieve by himself and he was not present when the risen Lord appeared to the other disciples. When Thomas finally returned and the others were talking about the resurrection, Thomas thought they had gone crazy. Perhaps, they were having hallucinations. A resurrection? Impossible! Thomas set his jaw and spoke his mind. He said: "Unless I see in his hands the print of the nails, and place my finger in the mark of the nails, and place my hand in his side, I will not believe" (John 20:25 RSV).

It was one moment of doubt that thrust Thomas into the role of being the disciple from Missouri. He was not going to believe just because others said so. He was saying, "Show me ..." the same thing you and I probably would have said.

The world has a way of forgetting the good things in a person's life and only remembering the mistakes. Shakespeare, in his play, *Julius Caesar*, said: "The evil that men do lives after them; the good is oft interred with their bones."

This is what happened to Thomas. There were many instances of his deep faith and commitment to Jesus Christ. But, that one moment of doubt has stuck with him down through the centuries. He has been saddled with the infamous label of Doubting Thomas or The Disciple From Missouri.

Today, as we look at this disciple from Missouri, I believe that we will discover that he had certain characteristics with which we can identify.

1. The Disciple From Missouri Was A Man Who Had Doubts.

A contractor said that he went out to check on a house he had built. The house was under the flight path for the airport and the woman told him that every time a plane flew over the house, the house would shake and their new home was literally falling to pieces.

Well, he checked all over the house for some kind of structural problem, but he could find nothing wrong. He told the woman,

"There doesn't appear to be anything wrong. It seems to be structurally sound."

The woman protested by saying, "Well, the house vibrates horribly every time a plane flies over. I'll guarantee that it will knock you out of the bed."

So, he stretched out on the bed and about that time, the woman's husband came in and asked, "What in the world are you doing in that bed?"

The contractor looked up at the angry husband and said, "I realize you may have some doubts, but would you believe that I am waiting on a plane?"

Doubt is a reality in every area of life — including faith. Just like Thomas, all of us, to some degree or another, have doubts in matters of faith. But, there is nothing wrong with having doubts. As you read throughout the Bible, you will read of men and women who wrestled with their doubts. The Psalmist cried out, "How long, O Lord? Will you forget me forever? How long will you hide your face from me?" (Psalm 13:1 NRSV). Job complained, "I cry to you and you do not answer me ..." (Job 30:20 NRSV). Thomas, the Disciple from Missouri, confronted with the news of the resurrection, said emphatically, "I will not believe unless I see for myself...."

A college student came by to see me one day. He was taking a required course in the Bible. He knew the stories of the Bible and had always taken them literally. But, as he studied biblical interpretation and form criticism and historical perspective, he was forced to admit that you cannot read the Bible strictly from a literal point of view. The Bible is a library of books, made up of many styles of writing. There are historical literature, biographical sections, poetic books, and allegorical books. All of the 66 books of the Bible are written to tell the truth and greatness of God's love, but you don't read poetry the same way you read history. And you don't read the wisdom literature the same way you read the parables of Jesus.

"I am so confused," this young college student said. "I've always believed everything in the Bible, but now I'm having doubts about what I believe. Isn't that awful?"

"No," I said, "I believe we all have doubts. If you don't have any doubts, you are either kidding yourself or you are sound asleep. Doubts," I said, "are the ants in the pants of faith. Doubts help keep your faith awake and growing."

Alfred Lord Tennyson was grief-stricken with the loss of his friend, Arthur Hallam. He was filled with doubt about God. But, after painfully working his way through the darkness of doubt, he wrote that beloved poem, "In Memoriam." He tells of his struggles with doubt and how his faith grew. He wrote:

You tell me, doubt is Devil-born.
I know not. One indeed I knew
In many a subtle question versed,
Who touched a jarring lyre at first,
But ever strove to make it true;

Perplexed in faith, but pure in deeds,
At last he beats his music out.
There lives more faith in honest doubt,
Believe me, than in half the creeds.

Doubt is not an enemy of faith, but a friend of faith. It is doubt that enables our faith to grow. It is doubt that enables our faith to struggle with doctrines and easy clichés. It is doubt that enables us to make spiritual progress.

Doubt is not a sin for which we should be ashamed, but an avenue for the achievement of a stronger faith.

2. The Disciple From Missouri Was A Man Who Was Committed To Jesus Christ.

History does not look at Thomas as one of the stained-glass disciples because of that moment of doubt. But, if Thomas had never doubted, he would never have believed. If Thomas had never doubted, he would never have been confronted by the resurrected Jesus who said to him: "Touch me ... prove it to yourself and believe ..." (John 20:27). If Thomas had never doubted, he would never have fallen to his knees and confessed: "My Lord and my God ..." (20:28).

24

Thomas moved from a position of doubt to a position of faith. It was the experience with the risen Christ that compelled him to move from doubt to commitment.

There are many of us who, like Thomas, are struggling in a world of doubt. We have gone off on our own and our faith has grown cold, and we are left wondering why our faith is not more vital.

There is an old cartoon about an elderly couple out for a Sunday afternoon drive. They were on a country road and a cuddling young couple in the car in front of them dramatically slowed their progress.

Finding it impossible to pass, the elderly couple began to talk. The little old lady looked across at her husband. Then she looked at the couple in front of them, who were sitting so close together. She asked her husband, "Why don't we sit like that anymore?"

Quick as a flash, her husband said, "I haven't moved."

Well, God hasn't moved either. If we don't feel that our commitment is as strong as it used to be, then we need to look within ourselves. This is the point! If we feel our faith has grown cold, if we feel alone, if we feel apart from God, then we need to look within ourselves and deal with the doubt that has moved us farther and farther away from God.

When Thomas was invited to see and touch the nail prints and the scars on Jesus, he no longer needed any proof. He quickly fell to his knees and committed his life to Jesus when he simply said, "My Lord and my God."

Tradition says that from this point on Thomas was committed to Jesus Christ. For the rest of his life, Thomas preached the gospel, and one tradition says that he was so committed to proclaiming the Good News of Jesus Christ that he died a martyr's death — telling of his experience with the risen Christ.

It is only when we are willing to commit ourselves to the risen Lord that our faith takes on any vitality. Prayer is never really meaningful until we fall at the feet of Jesus and feel his power in our lives. Forgiveness is never more than a word in a dictionary until we experience God's cleansing power for ourselves. Jesus is never more than a revered figure in history until we commit our hearts and lives to him. But, when we do commit our lives to him, we find a meaning, a purpose, and a direction for our lives which keeps us moving in the right direction.

Recently I officiated at a wedding. One of the groomsmen was the brother of the groom. He is a captain in the Air Force and flies with the Strategic Air Command. He is a navigator on a B-58, and his job is to guide the B-58, loaded with nuclear weapons, toward the Fail Safe point.

Apparently, it is a boring, monotonous job. I asked him if there was ever any excitement on those long trips. He said that dark and stormy nights are always exciting. They are exciting because you cannot see any shorelines or landmarks and your instruments can't be relied upon.

"So, what do you do?" I asked.

He said, "There is only one thing to do. When you can't see any landmarks and you can't trust your instruments, you climb above the clouds and get a fix upon the stars. Only then can you be sure you are going in the right direction."

Do you ever feel lost? Are you ever overwhelmed with doubt?

Whenever we feel like our lives have no real meaning or direction, we need to climb above the clouds of doubt and get a fix on the stars. We need to commit our lives to Jesus Christ and say as Thomas did: "My Lord and my God...."

When we do this, we will have discovered the best direction for our lives. We will have discovered One who helps us overcome our doubts. We will have discovered the One to whom we should commit our lives.

Have you struggled with doubts? Are you looking for direction in your life?

Perhaps, you need to get a fix on Jesus Christ. When you do, you will discover the direction for your life.

Prayer

Eternal God, we pray that you would give us the courage to walk with your Son. In his name. Amen.

Nathanael:
Do You Need An Alias?

John 1:43-51; 21:2

Several years ago, we were on a short vacation and went to one of the theme parks. In the park was a roller coaster that had enough turns and loops and drops to make it one of the most dangerous and frightening rides you have ever seen. It is so frightening and dangerous looking that it is hard to believe anyone would pay good money to ride it.

When we got off that ride, it was time to do something different. As we were going through the park, we came to a photographer's booth. But, this photographer was different. You could dress up in a variety of costumes and have your picture taken. My daughter selected a frilly dress with a boa to drape around her neck, and a hat with a large flower on it, and a fake beauty mark applied to her cheek.

My son, who was about ten years old, selected a Mexican blanket that pulled over his head, a belt of bullets to drape over his shoulder, a sombrero for his head, a rifle to hold, and a black patch to cover one eye. As he was examining himself in the mirror, the lady that was assisting him in putting on the costume asked, "Well, Jeff, what's your alias going to be?"

"What's an alias?" asked Jeff.

"An alias," said the woman, "is when you decide to go by another name. Since you are in a western costume, I thought you might have an alias that you would want to be called."

Jeff was silent for a moment and then said, "I think my alias will be 'Cactus Jack.' "

An alias is what the disciple Nathanael seemed to have. In the Gospel of John he is one of the first group of disciples. However, Matthew, Mark, and Luke do not list a disciple named Nathanael. Instead, they list another named Bartholomew. Most scholars agree that Nathanael and Bartholomew are the same disciple.

William Barclay, perhaps the most authoritative biblical scholar this past century, affirms that Nathanael is an alias for Bartholomew. He states that they are closely related in the biblical text. They are both closely associated with Philip and Bartholomew may have simply been a descriptive alias which identified him as the son of Talmai.

So, although there is no way to be absolutely positive because the proof falls short of certainty, one of the disciples of Jesus seemed to use an alias. The importance of this disciple, Nathanael or Bartholomew, was not in his name, but in his willingness to be a disciple of Jesus Christ. He saw in Jesus something that was worth giving his life to be one of Christ's disciples.

Today, as we look at this disciple with an alias, I want to lift up a few things that we know about this disciple.

1. The Disciple With An Alias Was Prejudiced.

When Philip came running to his friend and told him, "We have found him of whom Moses in the law and also the prophets wrote, Jesus of Nazareth," Nathanael simply sneered and asked: "Can anything good come out of Nazareth?" (John 1:46 NRSV).

Why was Nathanael so prejudiced against Nazareth? There is no rational explanation for prejudice. It is simply one of the evils that exist in the hearts of men and women. Nathanael came from Cana of Galilee, a small village about eight miles from Nazareth. Perhaps, Nathanael was simply speaking of the jealousy and prejudice which exists between small towns, and he was wondering how the promised Messiah could come from an unimpressive city.

We have the same kind of prejudice in our world today. I know a man who would be classified as a Sooner patriot. He literally lives and breathes Oklahoma football. He makes the pilgrimage every year to the annual Oklahoma vs. Texas football game in the Cotton Bowl. He very seldom has a good word for Texas. Well, you can imagine his surprise when he discovered that his company was transferring him to Dallas, Texas. He was further surprised to discover that his children had picked up on his prejudice about Texas.

On the night before they moved, he read his children a bedtime story and then listened to their prayers. His little boy prayed: "God bless Mommy and Daddy and Grandma and Grandpa. And I guess, God, this is good-bye because tomorrow we're moving to Texas."

We are not born being prejudiced, it is something that we learn along the way. We learn to be prejudiced from our family, our friends, and our neighbors. Consequently, over the years we have developed many deep-seated prejudices that color and distort our views of people, places, and events.

I don't want to sound holier-than-thou, but one of the things that I have very little tolerance for are jokes which cater to our prejudices. The joke may be funny, but if it is insulting to Blacks, to the Polish, to the Jews, to women, or to those of different sexual orientation, I have trouble with a prejudice indictment against a whole people.

I am sure that there have been many experiences of prejudice that we have observed, but there is one experience that had a profound influence in my life. I was about six or seven years old and I was visiting my grandparents in Hope, Arkansas. My grandmother took me shopping with her and I wandered off in the store to find a drink.

I found the water fountain, but I was too small to reach the spigot. A little African-American boy, about my age offered to boost me up so I could get a drink. I got my drink and then I boosted him up to get a drink.

Just about the time he started to get a drink, his mother came up and told him he couldn't get a drink out of that water fountain. He did not understand why, and he asked. She pointed to a sign over the water fountain that stated: "Whites only." She took him very firmly by the hand and started to walk away. As they walked away from that "Whites only" water fountain and me, I heard that little boy say to his mother, "Mama, I wish I was white."

That event took piace years ago, but it was an event that was burned into my heart and mind. Even though I was only a small child, I knew that it was wrong to treat other people as second-class citizens. I knew that all people should have an equal opportunity. I knew that all people are equally loved by God. I knew that all people should be treated equally.

There have been a lot of changes in attitudes over the last fifty years. But, there are still bitter prejudices buried deep inside our souls. Before Nathanael met Jesus, he was filled with prejudice. But, a change came when he met the Master. I believe that when we meet the Master — a change begins to take place within our lives. We move from hatred and bitterness and prejudice to seeing each person as a child of God! This is the essence of the Christian faith.

2. The Disciple With An Alias Was A Dreamer.

Nathanael followed his friend, Philip, to meet Jesus. As they approached him, Jesus saw Nathanael and spoke one of the greatest tributes that Jesus ever gave. He said: "Behold, an Israelite indeed, in whom is no guile" (John 1:47 RSV). Nathanael was surprised that Jesus even knew him and he asked, "How do you know about me?" And Jesus said, "I saw you under the fig tree" (1:48).

The fig tree was leafy and shady, and it was customary for devout Jews to sit under the cool branches of the fig tree to think and pray and dream about God's chosen One. There is no telling how many times Nathanael sat under that fig tree dreaming.

Nathanael was not satisfied with small or insignificant dreams. He dared to have important dreams. He dreamed about the coming of the Messiah. He dreamed about restoring Israel to its place of prominence among the nations of the world. He dreamed about doing his part in helping the expected Messiah establish his kingdom.

Dreams are the stuff of which life is made. The life that goes on in the mind — the good, the positive, the daring — has a way of becoming reality when we dare to try to make those dreams come true. Columbus dreamed and a new world was discovered. Edison dreamed and the electric light bulb lit up the darkness. Jonas

30

Salk dreamed and a deadly disease was brought under control.

Sister Theresa had a dream one day to build an orphanage. She shared the dream with her superiors and they asked the expected question, "Where will you get the money to build an orphanage?"

"Well," Sister Theresa responded, "I have three dollars."

"Sister Theresa," her superiors chided her, "you cannot build an orphanage with three dollars."

"I know," she said, smiling, "but I have a dream and I have three dollars and I have God. I can do anything."

Every great advance in human history has come about because someone dreamed a dream and dared to believe that with God's help it could come true. Do you have a dream? What are your dreams? Are you dreaming of a happy marriage? Are you dreaming about stopping smoking? Are you dreaming of losing weight? Are you dreaming of a good education and a promising career? Whatever your dreams, if you have God with you, then your dreams are possibilities.

3. The Disciple With An Alias Was A Person Of Faith.

The encounter with Jesus had a profound effect upon Nathanael. He was no longer content to sit idly under a tree and dream. This One called Jesus touched his soul. This One called Jesus looked inside his heart. This One called Jesus challenged Nathanael to become a disciple. There was something so irresistible about Jesus that Nathanael could not help saying: "You are the Son of God! You are the King of Israel!" (John 1:49 RSV).

Nathanael responded to Jesus with faith. And, in the twinkling of an eye, he moved from being a prejudiced dreamer to being a committed disciple. He gave his life faithfully following Jesus Christ.

Isn't this what we are called to do? Are we not called to walk in the footsteps of Jesus?

A few years ago, I was asked to edit a book about ministers. I spoke to several people about their call to the ministry, their decision to get a theological education, and their decision to commit their lives to follow Jesus Christ faithfully.

One minister told me he knew God was calling him into the ministry, but he ignored the call. He went to law school, he became successful as an attorney, and he was involved in the church and a lot of charitable organizations. But, on the inside of his heart, he knew that he was ignoring the call of God in his life.

Then, one Sunday morning, everything came to a head. He said:

> *I don't remember what the preacher spoke about that morning. When we stood to sing the last hymn, I felt that I needed to commit my life to following Jesus Christ. I could feel his gentle tugging upon my life. I could almost hear him softly whispering my name. I held on to the back of the pew so tightly that my knuckles were white. But God kept whispering my name and challenging me to follow him and I let go of the back of the pew and slipped down to the front and committed my life to following Jesus.*

Is Jesus whispering your name today? Is God calling you to the ministry? Is God calling you to be a Sunday school teacher? Is God calling you to be a better husband or wife? Is God calling you to be a better mother or father? Is God calling you to follow him faithfully as one of his disciples?

Listen! Listen very carefully! Is God quietly whispering your name and calling you to follow him faithfully?

Prayer

O God, help us to be aware of your Spirit speaking to our hearts and our lives — even now. And, give us the courage to respond to him. In his name. Amen.

James:
The Unknown Disciple

Matthew 10:3; Mark 15:40

It is fascinating to visit some of our historical landmarks in Washington, D.C., like the Lincoln Memorial, the White House, the Smithsonian Museum, and the U.S. House of Representatives and the U.S. Senate.

One place is very special. I do not think any one of us could walk through Arlington National Cemetery without experiencing a great deal of emotion. When you see row upon row of white crosses, you suddenly become aware that the real cost of our freedom has been bought and paid for in human lives.

In Arlington Cemetery, there is a special tomb which has an honor guard 24 hours a day. The honor guards come from every branch of the military services and they stand guard at the Tomb of the Unknown Soldier. They honor men and women who have died in defense of our freedom. They honor the soldiers and sailors and air force and marines who have been killed fighting for our freedom. In this Tomb of the Unknowns, as it is often called, there are the remains of unidentified members of the military from World War I, World War II, and the Korean War. In 1998 the body of the "unknown" Vietnam soldier was identified and moved and buried in his hometown.

This tomb is symbolic of all who have died in the service of our country. The inscription on the tomb is simple, yet poignant. It says: "Here rests in honored glory an American soldier known but to God."

As I have thought about the inscription on that tomb, I have realized that this could be said of many disciples of Jesus Christ. They are unrecognized in the affairs of the world. Many followers of Jesus are forgotten soldiers of the cross. They are unknown disciples of Jesus Christ.

The disciple we are looking at today is an unknown disciple of Jesus. Although we know his name, we know little else about him. His name is James and he is virtually invisible in the New Testament. The Bible does not contain a word he spoke or a deed he did.

However, we do know a few things about this obscure disciple. For instance, we know he was a short man because in one list of disciples he was called James the Less. His brother was Matthew because both are called sons of Alphaeus. He was a charter member of that band of disciples who changed the history of the world.

But, little else is known about James. A few oral traditions indicate that he was a Zealot and he had a heart filled with hatred against the Roman occupiers of Israel. Another tradition says he was sent by the disciples to preach in Persia and that he died a martyr's death because of his faith in the resurrected Jesus.

But, to be honest, we know very little about the disciple called James, son of Alphaeus. He has gone down through the centuries as an unknown disciple whose deeds and words and faith are remembered only by God.

Today, as we look at this unknown disciple in the Master's Cabinet, I want to look at some of the ways that we, too, are unknown disciples.

1. The Unknown Disciple Was A Follower.

Although there is no record of the words and deeds of James, we know that he was a follower of Jesus. Someway and somehow, James encountered Jesus and was invited to be a disciple. He never became a leader in that group of twelve disciples. He did not have the charisma of Peter. He never had the preaching power of the Apostle Paul. He never had the organizational ability of John Wesley or the theological mind of Martin Luther. James was a follower and he simply followed Jesus Christ with his life.

Every group needs its leaders — including the church. But, when there are too many chiefs and not enough Indians, there are problems. The hope of the church is to be found in the many people who are not leaders, but followers of Jesus Christ. They are people who live out their faith day in and day out.

A couple of years ago, the Chinese government and the rest of the world were surprised when they permitted the re-opening of some churches. For over forty years, the churches had been closed. The churches had been converted into warehouses. The pastors had been jailed or sent to re-education camps. The Christian churches of mainland China had been closed and presumed dead for years.

However, the Chinese government wanted to improve its image in the world and agreed to allow the churches to re-open. They fully expected the churches to be attended only by foreign visitors and embassy officials.

When the churches were opened once again, the Christians of China began going to church for the first time in years. The churches were packed and overflowing. The churches immediately went to several services to accommodate the crowds.

When some reporters asked a teary-eyed young Chinese woman, "You were obviously born after all the churches were closed. How did you come by your faith?" the woman replied, "I was raised in a home that loved God. Because of the dangers, we could not talk about our religion outside of the home and we could not go to church. But I was raised in an atmosphere of faith. I was not 'christened' in a church, but I was sprinkled from morning until night with the dew of religion. We never ate a meal without pausing to thank God. We never ended a day without Mother or Father reading a chapter from the Bible. As I was growing up, I very quickly discovered that God was never very far away."

I wonder if we are following Jesus Christ closely enough. Like the unknown disciple, we may not be leaders, but we can be followers of Jesus Christ. I believe that it is only when we dare to follow Jesus Christ that God's kingdom has a chance. We have to have bishops and ministers and leaders in the church, but we also need many more followers. James, the unknown disciple, was a follower and we ought to be followers also.

2. The Unknown Disciple Carried On The Work Of God.

To be honest, history records the exploits of the natural-born leaders. We know that Peter preached at Pentecost and 3,000 were converted. We know that Paul became the greatest missionary in the history of the church. We know that Matthew had a gift for writing, and he wrote an orderly account of the life and teachings of Jesus. We know that Thomas was a doubter and Judas a betrayer. But, what about James, the son of Alphaeus? We know his name and nothing more!

He was an unknown disciple who seemed to play a minor role among the ranks of the twelve. But, we know that he carried on the work of God. In the book of Acts, after the resurrection and ascension of Jesus into the heavens, the disciples met to choose a successor for Judas. James, the son of Alphaeus, is listed with the other disciples. He was still carrying on the work of God. He was still following Jesus. He was still doing what he could for God's kingdom.

The leaders of the gospel may get all the headlines, but it is the unknown disciples who are the backbone of the church. The Apostle Paul reminds us of this fact in the sixteenth chapter of Romans. He writes to the Roman church and says:

> *I send greetings to Priscilla and Aquila my fellow workers in the service of Christ Jesus; they risked their lives for me ... Greetings to my dear friend Epaenetus, who was the first man in the province of Asia to believe in Christ. Greetings to Mary ... Andronicus ... Junias ... Stachys ... Tryphaena ... Nereus....*
> — Romans 16:3-12 (TEV)

Paul lists 35 individuals in that one chapter, yet I doubt if we have heard of more than five or six of them. They are unknown disciples who carried on the work of God and Jesus Christ. Without their desire to carry on the work of the gospel and the church, the Christian faith might not have ever gotten beyond its infancy.

The unknown disciples have always been the backbone of the church. They were the people who lived out their faith, built the churches, taught the Sunday school classes, and made their religion so attractive that other people wanted it.

These unknown disciples may not be known in the affairs of the world, but they have carried on the work of the gospel and they have been used by God.

36

In the city of Boston there was a man named Kimball who was the manager of a shoe store. Very few people have heard of this unknown store clerk. Yet, it was he who introduced Dwight L. Moody to Jesus Christ. Dwight L. Moody became an evangelist, and years later a drunken baseball player named Billy Sunday was introduced to Jesus Christ. Billy Sunday became a preacher who introduced a YMCA official named Mordecai Hamm to Jesus Christ, and Mordecai Hamm, preaching in North Carolina, introduced a young man named Billy Graham to Jesus Christ.

Who was that shoe-store clerk? An unknown disciple who shared his faith and helped touch millions with the gospel!

Who have you shared your faith with recently?

It was a cold, snowy Sunday one winter in Kansas. The Methodist circuit rider could not make the journey out to a little country church. I do not know and I suppose that no one else remembers the name of the farmer who stood in the pulpit that Sunday morning. He was not dressed in a suit, but in overalls. His words were not polished oratory, but a simple sharing of what Jesus Christ meant in his life. But that day a young boy dedicated his life to Jesus Christ, and that young boy became Bishop William Quayle, who served his God and his church with distinction.

Who was the farmer? An unknown disciple who shared his faith in Jesus Christ!

Somewhere around 1920, a young newspaper reporter was assigned to cover a session of the Annual Convention of the Methodist Episcopal church meeting in Delaware, Ohio. He was upset at being assigned to do a story on religion. He would have rather been assigned to do a story on some crime, perhaps, investigate some alleged corruption, or even do a sports story, but religion just didn't interest him.

However, the reporter heard one layperson stand up and speak on an issue. In the process of speaking on this particular issue, the speaker quickly shared the meaning of his faith in Jesus Christ.

A hush came over the audience and the young news reporter was deeply moved. He left the church and walked the streets. He found himself praying: "O God, what is your will for my life?"

37

Gradually, he began to feel that his life was not to be lived as a news reporter, but as a minister of the gospel of Jesus Christ. And, he knew that if he was going to be a minister of the gospel, he needed a theological education.

So, he wired Boston Theological School and asked if there was an opening — an immediate opening. The school wired back a message which said: "HAVE PLACE FOR YOU. Stop. COME AS SOON AS POSSIBLE. Stop." Less than one week after that unknown lay person shared his faith, a young newspaper reporter named Norman Vincent Peale was entering theological school.

Who was that layperson? An unknown disciple who dared to share his faith!

These stories are fascinating stories. But, the most important people in the stories are not those with well-known names like Dwight Moody, Billy Sunday, Billy Graham, Bishop Quayle, or Norman Vincent Peale. Yes, these people with well-known names are important. But, the most important people in the stories are the unknown disciples who shared their faith in God.

You go back to the beginning of Christian history and you will find this unknown disciple. The unknown disciple is in back of every convert. The unknown disciple is in back of every Christian enterprise. The unknown disciple is in the back of every Christian movement in history — the obscure, the ordinary, the unknown disciple.

James, the son of Alphaeus, was a charter member of this grand and glorious group of unknown disciples. And the good news is that you can join the ranks of the unknown disciple when you live your faith each day, when you make your faith so winsome, so attractive, so meaningful in your own life that others say: "I want what you have!" "Your faith shall be my faith!" "Your God shall be my God!"

Are you ready to join the ranks of the unknown disciples? Are you ready simply to begin living your life with Jesus Christ in your heart?

Prayer

O God, may your light shine in us so that we may be useful examples of the faith we claim. In Jesus' name. Amen.

Peter:
Taking The First Step

Matthew 14:22-32

Recently, I had a very important meeting with my brother at The Ballpark in Arlington. He had two tickets to sit in one of the private boxes and watch the Texas Rangers play the Baltimore Orioles. I decided that sitting in an air-conditioned suite, with nice comfortable chairs, and an attendant to bring you barbeque, nachos, peanuts, pizza, or something to drink is the best way to go to a ballgame.

In the booth with us were about ten other people. One couple had a nine-month-old baby boy. He had a smile that could melt the coldest heart. He enjoyed being the center of attention, and he could pull himself up on the coffee table. It was obvious that he wanted to walk, but was afraid of letting go. His mother looked up at her husband and smiled. She said to him: "You know, it won't be long before he gathers up the courage and takes his first step."

One of the most appealing stories in the Bible is the one about Jesus walking across the water toward his frightened disciples. This passage is one of the most hotly debated scriptures in the Bible. Scholars argue about whether this text should be translated as walking "on the water" or "by the water." Quite honestly, I want to leave that debate to the scholars and focus on the disciple named Peter who was in the Master's Cabinet.

There is no passage in the New Testament in which Peter's character is more fully revealed. Peter was the loud, boisterous disciple. Peter was the disciple given to acting on impulse and often he acted without thinking about what he was doing. Peter was the disciple who was forever getting himself in trouble.

On this particular night, Jesus had gone up into the hills to pray and the disciples had put out to sea in a boat for some fishing.

Somewhere around three in the morning a storm blew up and began tossing the boat about in the waves. The disciples tried to row toward shore, but the strength of the wind and waves pushed them farther out. The harder they rowed, the more tired they grew. And soon, a little bit of fear began to creep into their hearts as they wondered if they would be able to survive the storm.

Then, in the very midst of their fears, they saw someone walking across the water toward the boat. They were terrified. They screamed with fear. Their superstitions convinced them they were seeing a ghost.

In the midst of their fears, Jesus called out to them and said: "Take heart; it is I; do not be afraid" (Matthew 14:27 NRSV).

As soon as they recognized the voice of Jesus, it was Peter who called out: "Lord, if it's really you, order me to come out on the water to you" (Matthew 14:28 TEV).

Three ministers went fishing: one Methodist, one Baptist, and one Catholic. The Baptist minister got out of the boat and walked on the water to the shore to get his fishing pole. Later, the Methodist minister got out of the boat and walked on the water to the shore to get some food. The Catholic priest said, "If the Protestants can do it, so can I." He stepped out on the water and sank. While pulling the Catholic priest out of the water, the other ministers asked, "Should we tell him where the rocks are?"

Now, try to put yourself in Peter's shoes and imagine how he must have felt. Impulsively, you have asked to walk across the water and Jesus invites you to come. Suddenly, you are overcome with doubts. You are thinking, "If I step out of the boat, I'll sink like a rock." You are aware that the other disciples are watching you and wondering just how big a fool you really are, if you are really silly enough to try walking across the water.

So, let's give Peter the credit for having the courage to take the first step. Peter gave up the security of the boat and stepped out into the unknown on faith.

Peter gave up the security of the boat and dared to try something that he did not know would work. Peter gave up the security of the boat and dared to take the first step across the water.

Today, as we look at this story, there are two things which I want to say about getting up the courage to take the first step.

1. Courage To Take The First Step Requires That We Stop Dwelling On Our Problems.

Before Jesus appeared to the disciples walking on the water, Peter had a more immediate concern. A storm was tossing their little boat across the waters. Fear was gripping their hearts. They were afraid that their boat might capsize. But, when Peter saw Jesus walking across the water, he forgot all about his problems for a few minutes. He forgot about his fears. He forgot about the winds. He forgot about the situation they were all in. He was so inspired after seeing Jesus walking across the water that he jumped out of the boat and began walking across the water to meet Jesus. Even though the fears later returned to Peter and he began to sink, for a few moments he stopped dwelling on his problems and discovered the courage within his heart to step out in faith.

Sometimes, we don't have the courage to take the first step into faith because we are so tied to our problems. The hurt that we feel is overwhelming. The pain that we feel may be devastating. The problems which we may be facing might seem to be insurmountable. When we dwell on our problems instead of the possibilities before us, we never have the courage to take the first step.

When I had an appointment out at one of the television stations, I noticed a worker climbing to the top of one of those high television antennas. Before going into the station, I stood and watched that man climb toward the top. I don't know how high one of those antennas reaches into the sky, but it was higher than I would want to climb.

I went into the station and had my meeting. Later, when I came out, the worker was coming down from the tower. I asked him, "How do you keep from getting dizzy climbing up so high?"

"Oh," he said, "it's really very simple. As I climb, I always keep my eyes fixed on where I'm going and not where I've been."

If we ever want to get the courage to take a step in a new direction for our lives, we must stop dwelling on our problems.

41

We must stop looking backward to where we have been. We must stop rehearsing our hurts and learn to look forward.

I know a man who came home from work one day and found a note from his wife. The note informed him that the children needed to be picked up at the nursery school. The note informed him that she has taken half of their savings from the bank. The note informed him that she had packed her belongings and was leaving him for someone else.

The young man was devastated. It seemed as though his whole world had fallen apart. The hurt he experienced in his heart and mind was greater than anything he had ever imagined. He began to drink — trying to drown his problems only to discover that his problems could tread water. He began to hate — only to discover that his hatred hurt himself more than anyone else. He began to grieve over the broken relationship, only to realize that his wife was not coming back.

Finally, at the urging of some friends, he went to church one Sunday. The minister's sermon was based on that text in Philippians 3:13-14 where the Apostle Paul says: "... forgetting what lies behind and straining forward to what lies ahead, I press on toward the goal for the prize of the heavenly call of God in Christ Jesus."

"It was at this point," the man said, "that I realized that I had to stop looking backward and begin looking forward. I knew the only way to get on with my life was to let go of the hurt and look toward the future."

This is something which we all need to learn. We will never have the courage to take the first step into our future as long as we are dwelling on the hurts and griefs and problems of the past. Do you have the courage to let go of the problems and hurts of the past and get out of the boat and take a step into your future?

2. Courage To Take The First Step Requires That We Remember That We Are Not Alone.

Whenever we read this story in the gospel, we usually think of the miracle as the walking on the water. However, the real miracle is the fact that Peter knew Jesus was there with him. When the first wave washed over his feet, when he began to sink beneath the waters, when fear brought forth a cry for help from Peter's lips as he cried out, "Lord, help me!" Peter was calling in the right direction — toward Jesus!

We are often compelled to leave the safety of our boats and walk into unknown waters. But, the Good News of the gospel is that we do not walk alone. Our God walks with us. Our God is there to comfort us. Our God is there to strengthen us.

I made pastoral calls for almost two years on a man who was dying with cancer. Visiting with him was not easy because it hurt to see a man not quite fifty years old suffer and grow weaker day by day. When I visited him in his home, we would talk for a while and then have a prayer together before I left.

As his strength declined and his pain increased, it was necessary for him to be hospitalized. Before entering his hospital room, visitors had to put on sterile gowns, face masks, and latex gloves.

Once, when I walked into his room, he looked up at me and asked, "Who is that masked man?"

One afternoon, before I left his room, I took his hand in mine and gave a prayer. When I said, "Amen." I started to withdraw my hand, but he held my hand securely in his. Then, he began to pray. There was not an ounce of self-pity or concern for himself in his prayer. He was not angry at God for allowing him to suffer. He was not praying for relief from his pain.

Rather, he was praying for me — his pastor! It was a moving prayer as he thanked God for using me to help him and his family. He thanked God for giving me the strength to do my work as a minister. He thanked God for the church and the way it had influenced his life. He thanked God for being with each of us, and he thanked God for the gift of his life.

As I walked out of the hospital to my car, I was thinking about what had just happened. A dying man knew that he was not alone. A dying man knew that there was One who walked with him. A dying man knew that even in the midst of his suffering and pain, the presence of God's love in Jesus Christ was with him.

Someone expressed this idea in an old song that says:

Just when I need him,
Jesus is near;
Just when I falter,
Just when I fear,
Just when I need him most,
Jesus is near.

There are thousands of people who can affirm that this is the real miracle. We may feel like we are walking into unknown waters, but there is One who knows our situation. There is One who knows our hearts. There is One who always walks with us.

Are you ready to take the first step?

Prayer

O God, give us the strength and courage to walk with you each day. In Jesus' name. Amen.

Thaddaeus:
A Rose By Any Other Name

John 14:19-24

One evening when the Archbishop of Canterbury, George Carey, was here, he wanted to get a Texas steak so I arranged to take the Archbishop out to McBride's Steak House.

During dinner, I was seated next to the Archbishop's wife and I called her "Mrs. Carey." She said, "Robert, my husband, is the one with the fancy titles. Just call me Aileen."

So, I smiled and asked, "Aileen, which of the fancy titles do you call your husband? Do you call him 'Archbishop'? Or, do you call him, 'Your Grace'?"

She looked at me and said, "Oh, Robert, you have a naughty sense of humor. I've called George many names, but I've never called him 'Your Grace'!"

Whether we are aware of it or not, names are important. Shakespeare said: "What's in a name? That which we call a rose by any other name would smell as sweet." But that is not true! Names are important because they identify people. And, a name can elicit an immediate response.

In today's scripture we are looking at one of the disciples in the Master's Cabinet who seemed to have several names. The preferred name is Thaddaeus. However, he is also called Lebbaeus. One other name that is used is a fairly popular name in Jewish history, the name Judas. Judas Maccabaeus was one of the great heroes of ancient Israel.

Consequently, the name of Judas was once an honored name. But, the name of Judas was disgraced when one of Jesus' disciples, Judas Iscariot, betrayed him. That is why when the writers of the New Testament refer to Thaddaeus by his given name of Judas, they always add, "not Iscariot." They wanted everyone to know that the Judas with the nickname of Thaddaeus was not Judas Iscariot who had betrayed his Lord for thirty pieces of silver.

The biblical writers knew that a name is important. A name identifies a person. A name may indicate something about our character. A name may indicate something about values in our life. A name may indicate something positive or something negative about us.

If you doubt this, just think about it for a minute. A man named Judas Iscariot betrayed his friend and his Master. His name is now associated with one who would sell his soul for a little silver or gold. A young woman named Monica Lewinski had a well-publicized affair with the President and her name is now associated with a sexual act. And a man named Jesus lived among us and taught us how to live and was crucified and resurrected, and those of us who follow him can claim the name of "Christian."

Thaddaeus was a quiet and inconspicuous disciple who was willing to give up all of his names in order to claim one name — one name which meant he was a follower of Jesus Christ, one name which indicated who he really was. He was a Christian.

What does it mean for us to claim to be Christian?

A rose by any other name may smell as sweet, but what does it mean for us to claim the name of Jesus Christ in our lives?

Today, I want us to think about this member of the Master's Cabinet — this disciple named Thaddaeus — and I want us to think about the difference it makes in our lives to be disciples of Jesus Christ.

1. It May Be A Rose By Any Other Name, But When We Claim The Name Of Jesus, It Should Make A Difference In Our Lives.

A lot of people claim the name of Jesus in their lives, but no one can tell. Their faith hasn't made any difference in their lives.

A man went to the doctor because he was tired and run down all the time. The doctor gave him a complete physical and then told him: "The best thing you can do is to stop smoking, stop drinking, go on a diet, start exercising, and stop carousing around town every night."

The man thought about this and then asked the doctor, "What's the second best thing I could do?"

Isn't this the way it is with many people who claim the name of Jesus in their lives? They know what is expected of them. They know that walking with Jesus requires them to walk with him each day, but they want to know if there is another way. They want to know if there is a way to talk the talk, but not walk the walk.

The evangelist Billy Graham tells about getting on the elevator at his hotel one evening. A man was already on the elevator. He had a party hat on his head, he had a drink in his hand, and he was so drunk, he could hardly stand up.

When Billy Graham and his wife stepped on the elevator, the drunk pointed at him and said, "I know YUZ! You're Billy Graham! You got me converted!"

Dr. Graham looked at the man and said, "Well, I must have converted you! It's apparent that the Lord had nothing to do with it!"

We have too many people who claim the name of Jesus in this way. They are willing to say, "I believe in Jesus." They are willing to tip their hats to God. They are willing to talk the talk, but they are not willing to walk the walk. They are not willing to allow Jesus to make a difference in their lives.

Do you know anyone like this? Are you like this?

Perhaps it is time we stop flirting with a commitment to Jesus Christ. Perhaps it is time we stop giving lip service to Jesus. Perhaps it is time that we stop pretending that Jesus is important to us. Perhaps it is time we allow Jesus to make a difference in our lives. Perhaps it is time that we seriously think about committing our lives to Jesus Christ so that it makes a difference in the living of our faith.

2. It May Be A Rose By Any Other Name, But When We Claim The Name Of Jesus, We Should Make A Difference In The Lives Of Those Around Us.

We cannot simply claim the name of Jesus on Sundays when we go to church. If we are living our faith, as we should, our faith should be making a difference in the lives of our family, our friends and neighbors, and our co-workers.

Thomas Wheeler is the CEO of a large insurance company. One Sunday afternoon, Tom and his wife took a drive out into the country. They were enjoying the beautiful countryside, and the animals in the field, and some quiet time together.

When they got low on gas, they pulled into an old, seedy-looking gas station. There was only one pump, so Tom got out to pump gas. While he was pumping the gas, his wife went to get them something to drink. He noticed that his wife was carrying on a friendly conversation with the gas attendant. He also noticed that when they finished talking, his wife gave the attendant a hug before she left.

When she got back in the car and they started to drive away, Tom asked, "Honey, did you know that man?"

She smiled and said, "Know him? Indeed I do. We dated in high school and even talked of marriage."

Well, Tom Wheeler couldn't resist bragging just a little bit. He said, "Boy, were you lucky I came along. If you had married him, you would be the wife of a man who runs an old dilapidated gas station instead of the wife of the CEO of an insurance company."

His wife smiled and said, "My dear, if I had married him, he would be the CEO of an insurance company, and *you* would be pumping gas."

That story makes a valid point. The way that we live our lives makes a difference in other people's lives. And, the way we live our faith should make a difference in other people's lives.

Are you making a difference in other people's lives by the way you live your faith? When people look at you, do they see someone who is constantly griping, constantly complaining, constantly criticizing? Or, do they see someone living their faith so attractively that it is making a difference in their lives?

48

3. It May Be A Rose By Any Other Name, But When We Claim The Name Of Jesus, We Need To Be Committed To The Church.

When we look at this disciple named Thaddaeus, we obviously do not know a great deal about him. We know that he was chosen by Jesus to be one of the members of the Master's Cabinet. We know that he lived his life faithfully following Jesus because he was still listed as a disciple after the crucifixion, and we know that he was committed to the church because tradition says that he died after being wounded by arrows while starting churches in Persia and Armenia. He was committed to the church.

Are you committed to the church? Are you committed with your prayers, your presence, your gifts, and your service?

One of my friends, Norman Neaves, tells of a couple who came to see him because they were having arguments about going to church. When they returned from their honeymoon, the wife said, "Let's go to church on Sunday!"

"But," the husband said, "I don't want to go!"

So, they argued all week. The next weekend, the husband was feeling guilty about his refusal to go the week before. He said, "Hey, let's go to church on Sunday!"

His wife said, "You wouldn't go with me last Sunday; I'm not going with you this Sunday."

Again, they argued all week.

Norman said to the couple, "You know, we never have that argument at our house. We made the decision a long time ago that when Sunday comes, we go to church! Decision made! No reason to argue!"

"But that's different," they said. "You have to go! You're the minister."

"Is it really any different?" Norman asked. "I know many committed Christian laypeople who never argue about whether or not they will go to church. They never even discuss it. They have already made the decision. One time many years ago. No excuses! No questions! No discussion! They will be there!"

Have you made that decision? Have you made the decision to be in church each week? Have you made the decision to support the church with your gifts? Have you made the decision to be committed to the church? Do you claim the name of Jesus in your life?

Remember, a rose by any other name may smell as sweet, but if you claim the name of Jesus in your life, he expects you to live like it. He expects you to act like it. He expects your faith to make a difference.

Prayer

O God, may the presence of Jesus Christ make a difference in our daily lives. In his name we pray. Amen.

Simon:
The Daring Gamble

Luke 6:15

Charles was a mover and shaker at one time in Washington, D. C. He was Special Counsel to the President of the United States. He was described as the "hatchet man" for the White House. He had publicly boasted that he would run over his own grandmother to advance his agenda.

Because of his involvement in the Watergate break-in and cover-up, Charles Colson was tried, convicted, and sent to prison. It was while in prison that Charles Colson had a spiritual rebirth. He accepted Jesus Christ as his Lord and Savior. There were some who were skeptical of his spiritual rebirth. There were some who snickered and made jokes. There were some who suspected a gimmick.

Today, more than twenty years out of prison, Charles Colson has answered his critics about how real his spiritual rebirth is. He is chairman of Prison Fellowship, a ministry he founded. He works to bring the Good News of Jesus Christ to prisoners and former prisoners to help them experience a spiritual rebirth and renewal of their lives. And when asked how this change in his life came about, Charles Colson smiles and says, "I dared to take a gamble on Jesus Christ!"

And this is what happened with one of the members of the Master's Cabinet — the disciple known as Simon the Zealot. The New Testament tells us almost nothing about Simon the Zealot except that he was one of the men Jesus chose to be a disciple.

However, since the title "Zealot" is attached to his name, we know that Simon was one of the hot-headed patriots sworn to resist the Romans by any means possible, including war, violence, and guerilla action. The Zealots were a group of assassins. They carried curved knives, and under the cover of darkness, they would use their knives on any Roman or any Jew suspected of collaborating with the Romans.

The Zealots were a group of renegade vigilantes who plundered and destroyed at the slightest provocation. Although they talked a great deal about brotherhood, they were mostly just hoods.

Simon was a member of the Zealots which meant that he was a fanatic, he was a revolutionary, and he had probably murdered a few Romans and Jewish collaborators. This is a reasonable assumption based on the people that Simon associated with on a daily basis.

The real question we must deal with when we look at Simon is: "Why did Jesus choose him?" "What did Jesus see in this man who practiced vigilante justice?" "Why did Jesus want a murderer to be one of his disciples?" "Why did Jesus dare to believe that Simon could change?"

Of course, we may never have the answer to these questions. However, the evidence is clear that Jesus' choice of Simon was a daring gamble to change a Zealot into a disciple.

Today, as we look at this disciple named Simon, I want to lift up some ideas relating to the daring gamble to change him from Zealot to disciple.

1. The Daring Gamble Sought To Change Hatred Into Love.

For the 2000 Summer Olympics Tommy Lasorda selected a group of baseball players to go and play baseball for the United States. These young men had never played together. They were up against powerful national teams like the Cuban team, which had won the gold medal in the last Olympics. And Tommy led the American team to a gold medal.

When asked how he did it, Tommy said that at the first team meeting he told them, "Gentlemen, we are going to Australia to represent our nation and we are going to win the gold medal. We are going to win because we are going to run, and hit, and throw. And, how are we going to do this? We are going back to the basics." Tommy paused, and playing off the old Vince Lombardi

52

coaching strategy, looked at the players and coaches and said, "Gentlemen, this is a baseball!"

Now, that is getting back to basics! And, getting back to basics is what Simon needs to do. He was so full of hatred and bitterness that he was of no use to anyone.

But, one day he found himself listening to a teacher named Jesus. He was invited to be a follower of Jesus. And Simon, not really knowing why, found himself as a member of the Master's Cabinet.

Slowly, Simon began to change. The hatred which gripped at his heart began to give way to love and forgiveness. He fell under the influence of Jesus and a change began to take place in his life. Hatred was changed to love and bitterness was changed to forgiveness.

Recently, I had a speaking engagement. After I finished speaking, I was standing around talking to some of the people. One of the men said, "Dr. Allen, if you have a moment, I would like to tell you something that happened to me last spring."

As soon as I was free, I walked over to a corner of he auditorium with this man. He said, "When World War II started, our unit was one of the first taken prisoner by the Japanese. Eventually, we were transferred to a prison camp in Japan. Most of our guards were pleasant, but there was one guard who was especially brutal. He would hit us with a rifle butt or kick us or mistreat us in some way. I hated that guard and I often daydreamed about being alone with him.

"Well," he said, "the war ended and I went home. For the next 55 years I tried to forget about that guard and the prison camp. Then, the Japanese government and the U.S. government arranged for a reunion of our Marine unit in Japan. Those old, dormant feelings of hatred for that one guard returned."

"Did you run into that guard?" I asked.

"Yes," the ex-Marine replied, "we were touring the city where the POW camp had been located and the Japanese government held a reception at the hotel. During that reception, this guard walked into the room. It was a shock to see his face, and tears formed in my eyes as I watched him approach. He stopped in front of me and asked, 'Do you remember me?'

" 'Yes,' I responded.

"Hesitantly, he stuck out his hand to me. It seemed to be in front of me for an eternity as the hatred and bitterness of years flooded my mind. Then, I slowly reached out my hand and took his.

" 'You have forgiven me?' the former Japanese guard asked. 'How is it that you have forgiven me?'

" 'Because,' I said, 'I am a Christian.' "

This is really the basics of our faith. If we are really going to be followers of Jesus, then we must dare to change the hatred and bitterness of past hurts into love and forgiveness.

2. The Daring Gamble Sought To Change His Enthusiasm Into Commitment.

Simon was enthusiastic in his belief that the Romans should be driven out of Israel. But, his enthusiasm degenerated into a fanaticism. He had a fanatical worship of the nation rather than of God. He was blinded by an enthusiastic prejudice which caused him to disregard other people in the world. His narrow, bigoted patriotism prevented him from seeing beyond the borders of Judea. Yet, three years of walking and talking and listening to Jesus Christ began to have an impact in his life. He grew in heart, mind, and spirit until he was changed from an enthusiastic revolutionary into a disciple who was enthusiastically committed to Jesus Christ. His enthusiasm was not diminished; it was simply transformed into a commitment to Jesus Christ that was so powerful that Simon sought to share his faith with people in Africa, in Persia, and in Great Britain. His commitment to Jesus Christ was so vital that he remained a loyal and devoted servant until he died a martyr's death.

Like Simon the Zealot, we are an enthusiastic people about many things. We are enthusiastic about our special football team, or some political issue, or our children's achievements. But, we often fall short in our commitment to God.

A couple of years ago, I attended a political convention. I sat in one of the bleacher seats and listened to some of the speeches by various people. There was one woman about twelve rows in front of me who was extremely excited about the convention. She was wearing a silly-looking hat with the name of her candidate printed on it. She carried some placards with his name and she waved them in the air. Every time her candidate's name was mentioned, she jumped up, yelled, and threw her hat in the air.

She was utterly convinced that her candidate was the best candidate. Then, she turned around and I saw her face for the first time, and she was a member of my church. I had never seen her that enthusiastic or that committed to God and the church.

I think the world is waiting for Christians to be really committed to Jesus Christ. I think the world is waiting for Christians to be committed in their speech, in their conduct, in their faith, in their love, and in their actions.

Just as Simon the Zealot was called to channel his enthusiasm into a commitment to discipleship, so are you! Perhaps you have felt his nudge in your life. Perhaps there is that uneasy feeling, the tugging at your heart to be committed to someone or something.

Could that not be Christ calling you to discipleship? Could that not be Christ calling you to commit your life to him?

Prayer

O God, enable us to see our opportunities to be your disciples. In the Master's name. Amen.

Philip:
Look Before You Leap

John 1:43-46

I know of an incident that happened a few years ago in New York City. Imagine in your mind the scene. It is the morning rush hour. The subway car is crowded with business people dressed in suits and carrying leather briefcases, and an unshaven man in a shabby-looking coat bumps into a man as the train pulls into the station.

Instinctively, the businessman feels his pockets and discovers his wallet is missing. When the subway doors open, the grubby-looking individual starts to step off the train when the businessman grabs his shoulders and says, "Give it to me!"

The man in the shabby coat gets a terrified look on his face. He lunges out of the subway car, and the businessman is left holding the shabby coat as the doors close and the train pulls out of the station.

The businessman realizes that everyone is watching him. He starts going through the pockets of the old coat and says to no one in particular: "Maybe ... maybe he put my wallet in his coat."

As he goes through the pockets he discovers they are empty! When he gets off the train, he tosses the old coat in a garbage bin. He goes to his office and calls his credit card company to cancel his cards and issue him new ones. He calls about getting another driver's license issued, and he borrows a few bucks from a colleague to make it through the day ... That evening, when he gets home, his wife says: "Honey, I've got dinner almost ready. I figured you would be hungry when I noticed that you left your wallet on the dresser this morning."

That is how problems start in our world. Someone leaps to a conclusion without pausing to think. Someone puts two and two together and comes up with five. Someone believes the worst about another without even pausing to check the facts. The most dangerous people in the world are those who decide too quickly, those who reach a conclusion based on faulty evidence, those who leap to a conclusion without looking.

One member of the Master's Cabinet, Philip, could never be accused of this fault. When Jesus said, "Follow me!" Philip was not quick to respond. Philip had to mull it over in his mind. Philip had to think about it. Philip withheld his answer until he had an opportunity to talk it over with a friend. And it was only after carefully looking and thinking that Philip dared to take the leap of faith.

Although Philip was a member of the Master's Cabinet, we know very little about him. His name means "lover of horses." He came from the little town of Bethsaida. He is not a very colorful individual, and each time we see him in the New Testament, he is being true to his nature of displaying caution.

Philip is a disciple that many of us can identify with because he is as totally human as we are. He is a man of solid worth. He is a man of strong character. He is a man of healthy caution. He is a man who knew it was important to look at a situation, to analyze the situation, and mull it over in his mind. Then, and only then, after he had looked at the situation very carefully, would he leap into anything new.

Today, there are a few things I want us to think about as we look at Philip and his tendency to look before leaping.

1. Philip Looked Before He Lept Because He Was Naturally Hesitant.

So often, when we look at these men who served in the Master's Cabinet, we want to make them out to be unique. We want to make them out to be extraordinary. We want to make them out to be holier-than-thou. We want to make them out to be saintly and religious. However, in reality they were just common and ordinary people who were fishermen and merchants and tax-collectors. They were people like you and me.

When we look at Philip, he was an individual who was naturally hesitant. He had trouble making up his mind on major issues.

58

Every time Philip is mentioned in the Bible, you get a clear picture of a man who was having trouble making up his mind.

When Jesus called Philip to be a disciple, Philip withheld his answer until he thought it over. When the Greeks came to Philip with a request to see Jesus, Philip would not make a decision until he talked to Andrew. When Jesus asked Philip how to feed the 5,000, Philip was hesitant to believe that it was even possible.

Philip's mind was not closed; he was simply reluctant to make a decision. This is also our problem. We want to keep looking and looking, but never leaping. There may be a decision to be made, but we are reluctant to decide. This is a common human failing.

General George McClellan was Abraham Lincoln's commander of the Union Army for a while. Lincoln kept urging him to go into action. Lincoln kept urging him to get his army moving. Lincoln kept urging him to engage the enemy.

But, McClellan kept waiting and waiting. He had several excuses. He was hesitant to make a decision and begin a battle. Finally, the President had enough and he sent a letter saying:

> *My Dear General,*
> *If you do not want to use the army, I would like to borrow it for a while.*
>
> Yours respectfully,
> A. Lincoln

It is very easy to postpone making a decision. We have a tendency to look and look and never leap. There is something very intriguing about just looking, but never deciding.

Aaron Burr was one of the greatest men in American history. He was the Vice-President of the United States. He ran for President on one occasion. And yet, his name is remembered as a traitor to our country. The turning point in his life came when he was a college student at Princeton University. It was during a religious emphasis week that a speaker challenged every person to open up his life to Jesus Christ.

Aaron Burr thought about that decision. It is said that he stayed up late that night, pacing the floor, thinking about opening up his life to Jesus. But, by morning, he still had not decided and he went on with his life. He faced the ultimate question of his life and he couldn't make a decision.

I believe that the most important decision that we have is in deciding whether or not we will accept God's love in Jesus Christ. But, we are cautious. We are hesitant about making such a decision. There are a lot of people who are procrastinating in the arena of faith. They are saying: "I don't know enough about the Bible." "I'm not good enough." "One of these days, I'll open up my life to Jesus." They are cautious. They are hesitant. They are adept in postponing their decision.

In the musical, *The Music Man*, the professor tries to get the librarian, Marian, to go out with him. She wants to go out with him, but she is hesitant and she keeps putting him off by saying, "Please, some other time. Maybe tomorrow."

The professor is persistent and keeps asking. But, after being put off again and again, he finally looks at her in exasperation and says, "Pile up enough tomorrows and you'll find that you have collected nothing but a lot of empty yesterdays."

This is what we do when we keep putting off our decision about Jesus Christ. We may be naturally hesitant about such an important decision. We may want to postpone our decision until we are more sure. But, all that we are doing is collecting a lot of empty yesterdays when we fail to make a commitment of our lives to Jesus Christ.

Have you been hesitant about making a decision within your life for Jesus Christ? Have you been looking and looking and looking, but remain reluctant to commit your life to him? Isn't it about time to stop looking and take the leap of faith by committing your life to Jesus Christ?

2. He Looked Before He Lept Because He Wasn't Going To Look Back.

A few years ago, I had a wedding and the young groom was extremely nervous. Now, most grooms are nervous, but this young man was so nervous that he kept pacing the hallway. He was wringing his hands. He was perspiring or sweating so much that rivulets

60

of perspiration were rolling down his cheeks and it was the middle of winter. Thinking he might be sick, I asked him, "Are you all right?"

"Yes, sir," he replied, "I'm fine."

"Well," I said, "you seem very nervous."

He smiled and said, "You know, I'm not just as enthusiastic about this marriage today as I was yesterday."

This is one of our worst faults. We make a decision for Christ, but there is very little enthusiasm. We give ourselves. We make a leap of faith. We make a commitment. Then, we have second thoughts. We look back and think, "Maybe I really was not ready to make that decision."

How often have you tried to second-guess one of your decisions? How often have you looked back and said, "Maybe I made a mistake." "Perhaps it was the wrong choice." "I wish I hadn't done that."

Most of us have a habit of looking back, and second-guessing is counterproductive to making our decisions work successfully. If we decide we are going to be Christians, then we can't look back. Once we choose Jesus Christ as our Savior, then we must look forward and live for him.

This is what Philip teaches us. He was slow in making his choice for Jesus, but once it was made, he would not look back. He became totally committed to Jesus Christ. He tried to live for Jesus.

When he told a friend about how Jesus touched his life, the friend, Nathanael, sarcastically asked, "Can anything good come out of Nazareth?" Philip did not argue with him; he simply said, "Come and see." Philip was so totally committed to Jesus Christ, his life had been so transformed, that he was not looking back, but telling others, "Come and see for yourself."

Philip became so dedicated to Jesus Christ that others could see something of Jesus in his life. Archaeologists, excavating the ancient city of Hierapolis, uncovered an ancient inscription in the ruins of a building which identified the building as a church. The inscription said: "The church of Philip, the Apostle of Jesus Christ."

Once Philip made the leap of faith, he did not look back. In spite of his shortcomings, he became so committed to Jesus Christ that others could see something of Jesus Christ in his life.

This is what we are called to do! We are called to make the leap of faith and become so committed to Jesus Christ that others see something of his love in our lives.

The church I pastored in Oklahoma City was fairly near the medical school. One young doctor was doing a rotation at Children's Hospital. He was assigned to care for a nine-year-old child. The child was running high fevers and would occasionally have a convulsion, and this young, inexperienced doctor was doing all he could to help this child. The child was frightened and sick. The doctor would talk to him and tease him. The doctor even found himself singing to help calm the boy down as he ran a series of tests to try to figure out what was wrong.

At one point, the little boy looked up at the doctor and asked, "Are you kin to Jesus?"

At that moment, the doctor realized for that one frightened child in the hospital, he had been the living presence of Jesus Christ.

Are you living in such a way that others can see something of Jesus Christ in your life?

Have you made that leap of faith by committing your life to him?

Prayer

O God, help us to make that leap of faith and begin following Jesus Christ in our lives. In his name. Amen.

James And John:
The Desire To Win

Matthew 20:20-28

A sports announcer was telling about the former coach of Ohio State, Woody Hayes, trying to recruit a particular player. He sat in the living room of this young man's house and outlined the advantages of playing at Ohio State.

When Coach Hayes finished his pitch, the young man's mother asked if she could say something. She explained that she would like for her son to attend Ohio State and to play football for Ohio State. And she would like for him to grow and mature in his football skills under Coach Hayes.

However, she told the coach, there would be certain conditions for her son to sign with Ohio State. Coach Hayes would have to change his offense to take advantage of her son's talent. Coach Hayes would have to be willing to start promoting her son for the Heisman trophy, and if the coach was willing to make these changes, she was sure that her son would help Ohio State win football games and maybe even the Rose Bowl and a national championship.

Coach Hayes stood up to leave and said to this mother, "Madam, I'm afraid Ohio State isn't the school for your son. However," Coach Hayes said with a smile on his face as he looked at the mother, "I would love to have you play tackle on our offensive line."

When somebody is running interference for someone, that tells you a great deal about them. When you love somebody, you want that person to win, you want that person to get ahead, you want that person to be successful.

The desire to win is within all of us. And this desire to win was in the disciples Jesus chose to follow him and be in the Master's

Cabinet. The desire to win was clearly in the hearts and minds of James and John.

James and John were part of the inner circle and along with Peter, they were the executive committee of the disciples. They were the ones closest to Jesus, and in all probability, James and John were cousins of Jesus because their mother, Salome, was the sister of Mary, the mother of Jesus.

In this passage, Salome and her two sons, James and John, came to Jesus. Salome said, "I want to ask you something." Jesus simply responds, "What do you want me to do?" Salome desires for her sons to be winners and the boys want the same thing. So, she asks, "Promise me that these two sons of mine will sit at your right and your left when you are King" (Matthew 20:21 TEV).

This is one of the most revealing passages in the Bible concerning the disciples. It is revealing because it tells that they still did not fully understand his mission. They were still thinking in terms of their own place in his kingdom. They still saw his kingdom as being here on this earth and they had a desire to win. They wanted a place of personal prominence. They wanted a reward for their loyalty. They wanted their ambitious desires fulfilled.

There is something within all of us that wants to win or succeed in life. It is not that we want to cheat the other person, but the desire to succeed, the desire to win, the desire to be first, this is a desire which is within each of us. Surely we know that!

Today, I want to look at this desire to win and lift up several things which I believe are important.

1. If You Have A Desire To Win, You Must Be Aware That Selfishness Can Be Destructive.

Salome asks for her two sons that they might sit beside Jesus when he comes into his kingdom. She asks that one might sit on the right and one on the left. These were the positions of honor, prestige, and power. Now, there is nothing wrong in desiring these positions of power providing you want them for the right reasons, providing you have earned them, and providing you honestly deserve them. But James and John requested the positions of power for purely selfish reasons. After all, Jesus had already looked at

Simon Peter and said, "You are Peter and upon this rock I will build my church."

These two brothers were clearly hurt that Jesus had promised a place of importance to Peter. They considered Peter to be a man of lesser ability than themselves and they decided to approach Jesus with this bold request. Their desire to succeed and be the ones with power in his kingdom became their dominating ambition and it caused conflict within the ranks of the disciples.

Selfishness caused hard feelings among the disciples and selfishness will bring destruction to any life. When the desire to win leads to selfishness, it will destroy you personally. It will destroy your family. It will destroy your business. It will destroy you because it destroys relationships.

John Dean, in his book *Blind Ambition*, describes his three years as special counsel to President Richard Nixon. He said, "For a thousand days, I would serve as counsel to the President. Shortly after being offered the position, I soon learned that if I wanted to make my way upward, into a power of confidence and authority, I had to travel downward through factional powers, corruption, and finally, outright crimes. Slowly, steadily, selfishly, I would climb toward the moral abyss of the President's inner circle of power until I finally fell into thinking I had made it to the top just as I began to realize that I had actually hit rock bottom."

The desire to win or succeed is normal in life. However, when a blind, selfish desire takes control of our ambitions, it can be a destructive factor in our lives. Just when we think we are on the road to success, we discover that our selfishness has brought destruction to our lives.

2. If You Have A Desire To Win, You Must Be Aware That What You Desire Cannot Be Given To You.

Look at how Jesus responded to Salome. She asked that a place of prominence, power, and prestige be given to her sons. Jesus leveled with her when he said: "Salome, I can't give this to your sons. You want them to have power and prestige and position. But, I can't give it to them because it is not mine to give" (John 20:22, 23).

This is true with everything in this world of real quality and real substance. You may desire something with everything that is within you, but no one can give you anything of quality. People can give you opportunity, material items, their heirlooms, and all kinds of things that have economic value, but no one can give you happiness or joy or anything of real quality.

In his autobiography *Mick*, former New York Yankees superstar Mickey Mantle told about playing one-on-one basketball with his fourteen-year-old son. One day the boy became so upset at losing to his father again that he went into the house crying.

Naturally, his mother, thinking he might be hurt, asked him what was wrong. The boy, still sobbing, finally said, "Daddy beat me again!"

Well, this boy's mother turned to her husband and said, "I hope you are proud of yourself, you big bully. You ought to feel really big about beating a fourteen-year-old boy in basketball."

After she finished her little lecture, he said, "Listen, honey, he may be crying because he wanted to win so badly and lost. However, the day is coming when he is going to beat me in one-on-one basketball. He is talented and one of these days he is going to win — really win. Then he is going to come running in the house shouting, 'Mom, I beat Dad!' And you are going to be so proud of him. But, most important, he is going to be proud of himself because he will have deserved to win."

Anything of real quality in this world cannot be given to you. That's what Jesus was talking about when he said: "James and John and Salome, you don't understand. You are asking me to give you something I can't give you. No matter how much you desire and want it, I can't give it to you."

3. If You Have A Desire To Win, You Must Realize That You Are Called To Serve.

The request of James and John annoyed the other disciples and a veil of animosity and resentment fell over the disciples. They were angry with James and John. They did not see why the two brothers should have the place of importance. They were plotting how they could stake out their own claims to power and prestige in Jesus' kingdom.

Jesus knew what was going on in the hearts and minds of the disciples. He knew the emotions which lurked just below the surface, so he called the disciples together and he spoke to them the words which are the foundation of the Christian life. He told the disciples that if they really desired to win, if they really wanted to achieve greatness, if they really wanted to have power in his kingdom, then they must learn to be servants. Jesus put it so simply: "If one of you wants to be great, he must be the servant of the rest; and if one of you wants to be first, he must be your slave — like the Son of Man, who did not come to be served, but to serve ..." (Matthew 20:26-27 TEV).

According to Jesus, the badge of success is not in the position you hold, or the size of your bank account, or the number of people who are at your beck and call.

The real winner is the one who is willing to be a servant. Jesus completely reverses the standards of the world and says that real winning is serving. Real winning is in helping others.

Roman Turski was a Polish flight instructor before World War II, and he was to fly a plane from Vienna, Austria, to Warsaw, Poland. As he was leaving his hotel room, a man came running desperately down the hall pleading, "Gestapo! Gestapo! Please help me!"

Even in the days just prior to World War II, Roman Turski knew who the Gestapo were. So, he opened his room door and told the frightened man to get in the bed and under the covers and to be perfectly still. Then, Turski rumpled the bed covers up so that it looked like he was just arising from his night's sleep. He took off his clothes and sat on the edge of the bed in his underwear.

Sure enough, the Gestapo knocked on the door and asked to examine his papers. Then, they left without searching the room. When they had gone, Turski said to the little man hiding under the covers, "You can't stay here. Come with me and I will fly you in my plane to a safe place."

So, Roman Turski flew the frightened man to Switzerland before flying on home to Warsaw. A few months later, the Germans invaded Poland and Turski escaped to England and joined the British Royal Air Force. One day, his plane was badly damaged in an aerial dogfight and he crashed as he was attempting to land. He was rushed to the hospital with severe head injuries and he was in a coma. The doctors did not see how he could survive. Later, when he finally awoke, he saw a face that looked vaguely familiar. "Remember me?" the man asked Turski. "You saved my life in Vienna and flew me to Switzerland."

"How did you find me?" Turski asked.

"After you dropped me off in Switzerland, I eventually made my way to Great Britain," the man said. "Yesterday, the papers carried the story of a Polish hero shooting down five enemy planes in one day before crash-landing. The papers said you had a serious head injury and I came to be with you."

"But why?" asked Turski. "Why would you want to come to be with me here?"

"Because," the man said, "I thought I could do something to repay you for helping me." The man paused for a moment and then said, "You see, I'm a brain surgeon, and I operated on you this morning!"

Give of yourself freely and generously in service to others and you can bet your life that you will have discovered the real secret to winning. When you really care about people, when you are really serving people, you will discover real greatness and it will feel like winning.

Do you have a desire to win? Jesus put it so simply when he said: "If you want to be great — you must be a servant of all."

Prayer

O God, help us to learn the art of greatness by our willingness to be your servants in our world. In Jesus' name. Amen.

Judas:
When Others Betray You

Matthew 26:14-16, 47-50

In history there is a long list of people who have betrayed their family, their friends, or their country.

Julius Caesar was on his way to the Roman Senate when he was attacked by his political enemies. Each attacker was to thrust a dagger into Caesar. Caesar stumbled and staggered away in the direction of a friend. Then he saw the dagger in the hand of his friend, and he asked, "Et tu, Brute? Even you, Brutus...."

The Military Academy at West Point has a Hall of Generals. In this hall, there is a plaque for each of our nation's generals with the battles listed on the plaque in which they fought. However, there is one plaque which has no name. It is the plaque of a Revolutionary War general who won the battles of Saratoga and Quebec. But, Benedict Arnold betrayed his country, and his name is not listed in the great hall of generals. The name of a traitor will not be listed beside those who helped to win and preserve our freedom.

But, the best-known betrayal in the history of the world is the betrayal of Jesus Christ by one who was a friend, one who was a disciple, one who was invited to be a member of the Master's Cabinet, one who served as the treasurer of the Master's Cabinet — a man named Judas Iscariot.

By taking the thirty pieces of silver and placing the kiss of death on the cheek of Jesus, Judas became known as the chief of the betrayers.

Why did Judas betray Jesus?

There are many theories. Some have said that he did it for the money — the thirty pieces of silver. Some contend that Judas did it because God had foreordained it and Judas was simply doing what God made him do. Some insist that Judas was simply wicked and he did exactly what he chose to do simply because he was not a person of very good character.

I think Judas betrayed Jesus because Judas was convinced that Israel's only hope to get rid of the Romans was to force Jesus to become a military leader. He wanted to force Jesus to defend himself. He wanted to force Jesus to use his personality and his presence to rally the Jews to a holy war to throw the Romans out of Israel.

I can justify this claim by looking at the Greek word used when Judas identified Jesus with a kiss. The normal Greek word for "kiss" is *philein*. However, the word used to describe the kiss Judas gave Jesus is *kataphilei*, which means to kiss fervently, excitedly, and with expectation.

Was Judas trying to force Jesus to act as a military leader? Was Judas expecting Jesus to lead a nationalistic revolt?

We may never know. After the kiss to identify Jesus, Judas vanishes from the scene. Judas does not appear as a witness at the trial. Apparently, Judas staggers away, realizing how he had miscalculated Jesus, realizing that he, Judas Iscariot, regardless of his motives, had betrayed his Lord.

And Judas reappears on the scene to throw the thirty pieces of silver at the feet of the chief priest. Then he went out and hung himself — the final indication that his plan had gone wrong.

There is something in all of us that understands betrayal. We have had family and friends betray a confidence. We have had family and friends betray us with a lie. We have had family and friends betray our love. We know what it is to be hurt. We know what it feels like when others betray us.

So, what do we do? How should we respond when someone betrays us?

Today, I want to suggest three things we can do when someone betrays us.

1. When Someone Betrays You, You Will Have To Decide How To Respond.

When someone betrays you, the hurt is real. You did not want to be betrayed. You did not want to be hurt. You probably didn't even do anything to deserve being treated the way someone is treating you.

So, what do you do? When someone has made life for you a living hell, what do you do?

You have to make a choice!

Several years ago, when I arrived in Oklahoma City, we had a beautiful Gothic sanctuary. For some reason, we had flocks of pigeons which nested above the front door. Needless to say, the mess on the front steps was awful. You had to tiptoe through the tulips, as it were, to come into the church and you were in danger of getting your Sunday-go-to-meeting clothes soiled. Consequently, the custodial staff had to get out a power sprayer to clean the steps and he would blast the birds with water to run them off. But, how do you keep the birds away?

Someone suggested we shoot the birds. But, that was against the law. Besides, would you want to see your church on the evening news under the lead-in of "Methodist Church slaughters birds!"?

Someone else suggested we have the ushers stand out on the front steps with a towel in their hands and wave them in the air to keep the birds away. Can't you imagine what people driving by would have thought with the ushers standing out there waving towels? They would have thought, "Those Methodists have the strangest rituals!"

One Sunday, my son and I arrived at the church early. I opened the front door and a pigeon flew into the narthex. We tried to shoo him back out the door, but all he did was fly around and around the narthex. In a little bit, he was exhausted, he landed in the corner, and I went over and picked him up.

What would you do with a bird that was causing you problems? Would you wring its neck and say, "One down — 100 more to go"? Would you save him for the ushers?

But, do you know what I did? I walked outside and tossed him in the air and thought, "If you have to go to church, go to the Presbyterian Church down the street."

Life is kind of like that. You get mad at something or someone, you have trusted someone and they have hurt you, sometimes someone has given you hell, and you think about doing a lot of

71

things. But somewhere along the way you have to make a choice. You have to decide how you are going to respond.

2. When Someone Betrays You, Don't Try To Get Even.

When we have been hurt — betrayed — it is only natural to want to get even. I've even seen a bumper sticker on a car which said: "Don't Get Mad; Get Even." And we understand that philosophy. When we have been hurt in any way, we want to strike back.

One Sunday, I was standing at the back of the church visiting with people. A woman who had been watching our services on television had visited that Sunday. When I greeted her, she said; "Robert, I just wanted to tell you that you surely do look a lot better on television than you do in person!"

Now, what do you say to that? Do you strike back and get even? I thought, maybe her words came out wrong. So, like an idiot I said, "Excuse me, what did you say?"

So, in an even louder voice, this woman looked at me and said: "You surely do look a lot better on television than you do in person!"

There are going to be times in your life when someone deliberately does or says something that cuts you to the quick: you will feel betrayed, you will feel hurt, you will feel like striking back, you will feel like getting even, and you will feel like hurting them because they hurt you.

But, this is not the way of Jesus. He taught that forgiveness is better than vengeance. And, he was right! I don't know of anything more powerful or more life-giving then forgiveness.

Dr. Paul Scherer, the great Lutheran preacher, found himself on the opposite side of a certain social issue than Harry Emerson Fosdick. Paul Scherer attacked Fosdick's position and he also attacked Fosdick personally. As a result of this conflict, Paul Scherer was later embarrassed that he had betrayed a friend and colleague with such a harsh personal attack.

Some months later, Dr. Scherer was at an event at Union Seminary. He saw Harry Emerson Fosdick come in the room and he wanted to leave. Dr. Scherer describes what happened:

At that moment, Dr. Fosdick put his hand on my shoulder and gave it a gentle squeeze. He said nothing. He just squeezed my shoulder ... As a result of that moment, Harry Emerson Fosdick and I became the closest of friends. His forgiveness was stronger than ... vengeance.

The power of forgiveness is incredible!

Jesus taught us by word and example that getting even is not the best way. He taught us that forgiveness is better than vengeance.

3. When Someone Betrays You, Remember That Love Is Better Than Hostility.

The way of Jesus is the hard way. When we have been hurt, when someone has betrayed us, it is only natural to want to strike back ...

But, Jesus, in his life and teachings, challenged us to a different way of responding. He challenged us to remember that love is better than revenge. Love is better than an "eye for an eye." Love is better than returning evil for evil. Love is better than hostility.

At a board meeting of a children's home, the devotional was given by someone who told about a freckle-faced ten-year-old boy named Tommy. He had been at an orphanage for almost six years. Adoptive parents came and visited. They looked at the children, but no one seemed to want to adopt Tommy.

One day, a couple pulled up to the orphanage in a chauffeur-driven limousine. The director sent for Tommy and he was told this couple wanted to adopt him.

The well-dressed woman smiled at Tommy and said, "Tommy, if you come home with us, you will have more than you ever dreamed possible. You will have your very own room, new clothes, new toys, and we might be able to get you your very own pony."

Surprisingly, Tommy said, "Well, if that's all you have to offer, I'd just as soon stay here."

A bit surprised, the director of the orphanage asked, "Tommy, what more could you want?"

Tommy looked up at him and the couple who wanted to adopt him and said, "I just want someone to love me."

More than anything, this is what we see in the Spirit of Jesus Christ. I've always believed that if Judas had not hung himself, if Judas had waited a few days, if Judas who betrayed his Lord had gone with Peter who denied his Lord, together they would have discovered a risen Lord who loved them instead of hating them. Together they would have discovered a risen Lord who loved them and challenged them to "feed my sheep."

Do you know why I believe this? I believe it because the power of love is the strongest thing of all. I believe it because the power of love is stronger than evil. I believe it because the power of love is stronger than hostility.

You, too, can make this discovery when you decide to follow Jesus Christ as one of his disciples.

Are you ready to follow him? Are you ready to join the Master's Cabinet?

Prayer

O God, help us to keep our promise to walk with you — even when we find ourselves being pulled in different directions. In Jesus' name. Amen.

The Cost Of Discipleship

Luke 14:25-33

One of the undeniable marks of a great leader is that he makes his expectations very clear. Garibaldi, the Italian patriot, said to those who would follow him:

> *Soldiers, what I have to offer you is fatigue, danger, struggle, and death, the chill of the cold night in the free air, and heat under the burning sun, no lodgings, no munitions, no food, but forced marches, dangerous outposts, and continual struggle with bayonets against artillery. Those who love freedom and their country may follow me.*

In the dark days of World War II, when the British were standing alone against Hitler and his Nazi empire, Prime Minister Winston Churchill addressed the nation on the BBC by saying:

> *We shall fight on the beaches. We shall fight on the landing grounds. We shall fight in the fields and in the streets. We shall fight in the hills. We shall never surrender....*

King Arthur would bind his Knights of the Round Table with vows of allegiance so strong that someone said:

> *He bound his knights by vows so straight that when the knights rose from kneeling, some were pale as at the passing of a ghost. Some flushed, and others dazed. As one who wakes half-blinded at the coming of the light.*

But, no one demanded more of his followers than did Jesus. His terms of discipleship have been called startling — even harsh.

No leader ever demanded more of his disciples than did Jesus when he said: "If anyone comes to me and does not hate his father and mother and wife and children and brothers and sisters, yes, and even his own life, he cannot be my disciple. Whoever does not bear his own cross and come after me, cannot be my disciple" (Luke 14:26-27 RSV).

That is being pretty straightforward. Evidently, people were flocking to Jesus as his fame spread. The inquisitive came to watch like those who go to watch a fire. The self-seeking came to make their fortune on his popularity. The revolutionaries came looking for a military leader who would help throw off the shackles of Rome. Many people were moved to follow him because of the impulse of the moment, but they did not know what following him might mean for their lives. So, Jesus lays out the cost of discipleship, and his costs of discipleship staggers the crowd of people.

Then Jesus tells two parables of a rash king and a rash builder. In the parable of the rash builder, Jesus was making fun of builders who start extensive towers but then run out of money and leave the towers unfinished.

Jesus was challenging his followers to count the cost. Can you live by the demands of the Ten Commandments and the Sermon on the Mount? Are you willing to pay the cost of stewardship and commitment? Are you ready to follow Jesus? Will you count the cost before you decide to be his disciple?

In the parable of the rash king, Jesus tells of a wise king who counts the cost, appraises the odds, and does not rush headlong into battle. Jesus is reminding us that a wise person will carefully examine the conditions and cost of discipleship before making a decision to follow him.

In these stories, Jesus was challenging you and me to be aware of the cost of discipleship if we are going to join the Master's Cabinet as modern-day disciples. Have you counted the cost of discipleship? Today there are three things I want to say.

1. Discipleship Demands That We Put Jesus First.

Dietrich Bonhoeffer claims that churches have made the term of discipleship into what he calls "cheap grace." He writes:

Cheap grace is ... letting the Christian rest content with his worldliness ... instead of following Christ ... Cheap grace is the preaching of forgiveness without requiring repentance, baptism without church discipline, communion without confession, absolution without personal confession, cheap grace is grace without discipleship, grace without the cross, grace without Jesus Christ....

It is easy to document the spread of cheap grace. We have seen people join the church because they simply want their names on the roles for purposes of marrying and burying. We have seen people join the church in moments of emotional need and once the crisis is over, their commitment is over. We have seen people join the church because they thought something was in it for them. This is cheap grace! This is discipleship without commitment! This is discipleship without cost!

The cost of being a disciple of Jesus Christ is clear. It is putting Jesus first — first in our stewardship or use of our money, first in our commitment, first in our daily lives. Jesus must be first in our lives so that others can see Jesus in us.

A missionary couple left their twelve-year-old son with his grandparents while they went to India to begin their mission work. Their intention was that once they were settled, they would send for him. But, shortly after they arrived in India, World War II broke out. They were separated for four years — four years of no contact, of no letters or phone calls, of worry and concern. Then, there came a day when the war was over and the missionary couple could return home. The son writes about seeing his parents for the first time:

When the train pulled into the station, my mother was the first off the train. We embraced in the semidarkness. Then she took me by the hand and led me into the light of the waiting room. There were tears streaming down her cheeks as she looked at me ... Then she turned to my dad and said, "Albert, he's gone and looked like you. He looks just like you!"

This is what happens to us when we begin putting Jesus first as one of his disciples. We become so much like him that others see Jesus in us. Others look at us and become aware of God's love in Jesus Christ. Others look at us and see the presence of Jesus Christ living in us.

Let me ask you a hard question. When that day of judgment comes for your life and Jesus looks at your record as a disciple, your stewardship record, your level of commitment, whether or not you lived so others could see him in your life, what do you think he will say to you? Will he say, "Well done, good and faithful servant"? He will if you live your life putting him first.

So, are you willing to do it? Are you willing to put Jesus first? Are you willing to live in such a way that others can see Jesus Christ in your life?

2. Discipleship Demands Self-Denial And Maybe Suffering.

Jesus said, "Whoever does not bear his cross and come after me, cannot be my disciple." A person carrying a cross was a cruel and familiar sight to those who heard Jesus. He was telling them that self-denial and suffering may be part of the cost of discipleship.

One of my favorite books is Harper Lee's *To Kill A Mockingbird*. She describes a Mrs. Dubose who took morphine as a painkiller. As the last months of her life were passing, she knew she was an addict. She wanted to break her addiction and leave this world "beholden to no one or no thing."

So, she quit cold turkey and endured the pain and the craving for drugs because she wanted to free herself. During this time, Atticus Finch sent his son Jem over to her house each afternoon to read to her. It was a disagreeable job for the boy because the pain made her cantankerous, rude, and ungrateful. When she eventually died, Atticus Finch explained to his son why he was sent over to read every afternoon. He said:

> *I wanted you to see something about her. I wanted you to see what real courage is ... Real courage is when*

you know you're licked before you begin, but you be-
gin anyway and you see it through no matter what.
You rarely win, but sometimes you do. Mrs. Dubose
won, all 98 pounds of her. According to her views, she
died beholden to nothing and nobody. She was the brav-
est person I ever knew.

The witness of such suffering and self-denial challenges us
with the demands of discipleship. We are required — notice that
word, "required" — to be willing to deny ourselves, to be willing
to endure suffering, to be a disciple of Jesus Christ.

Philip Hallie tells of a village in France called Le Chambon
which hid Jews from the Nazis and smuggled them into Switzerland, even at the risk of their own lives and the lives of the people in
the village. One woman in the village, telling how it all began said:

A German woman knocked on my door. It was in the
evening and she said she was a German Jew ... She
was in danger ... Could she come into my house? I
said, "Naturally, come in ... come in!"

It happened that simply. "Naturally," she said at the possible
cost of her life, her family's lives, and perhaps even the whole
village's life.

This is what discipleship demands! We must be willing to pay
the cost of suffering and self-denial by simply saying, "Naturally
... come in ... come in."

3. Discipleship Demands That We Live In Relationship To Jesus Every Day.

It was a distinguished Hollywood party which had all of the
"beautiful" people present. It was a party that you went to just to
be seen. The hostess asked an actor to give a dramatic reading.
Instead of choosing something from Shakespeare, he gave a dramatic reading of the Twenty-third Psalm. The words flowed elo-
quently from his lips. The charm of his voice made those words
come alive, and there was a generous applause when he finished.

Then, the actor invited an elderly minister to read the same Psalm. He did not need the written script to repeat the words, he repeated them from memory: "The Lord is my Shepherd, I shall not want ..." but the words were so meaningful that many people had tears in their eyes.

The actor stepped to the podium once again and said, "I merely read the Psalm, but he knows the Shepherd of the Psalm."

This is the real mark of a Christian disciple — not that we merely know about Jesus, but that we know him and live in relationship to him every day. One of our basic mistakes is to think of Jesus as someone who lived many years ago. He should not be simply a figure in a book, but a living presence in our lives today and every day. Being a disciple is not merely a Sunday morning event, but a relationship which is nurtured and growing every day.

Hartzell Spence grew up as a preacher's kid. His father was a distinguished pastor and president of Morningside Methodist College in Sioux City, Iowa. In his book, *One Foot In Heaven*, his father says to him:

> *The thinking of the church has come a long way. When I became a preacher, there were a lot of don'ts! But, today, Christianity has become something to live each and every day, not just something reserved for Sundays.*

Yes, discipleship demands that we live in relationship to Jesus each day. Are you doing this? Are you willing to pay the cost of discipleship?

Jesus made it plain what it would cost to be one of his disciples. Are you willing to pay the cost?

Prayer

O God, prevent us from rashly or foolishly knowing you. Help us to count the cost. Help us to weigh the facts. Then give us the courage to live for him every day. In Jesus' name. Amen.